How to
Quit Smoking
without Gaining
Weight

Books by Martin Katahn, Ph.D.

The Rotation Diet Cookbook
(with Terri Katahn)

The T-Factor Diet

The T-Factor Fat Gram Counter
(with Jamie Pope-Cordle)

One Meal at a Time

The Low-Fat Fast Food Guide
(with Jamie Pope-Cordle)

The 200 Calorie Solution

Beyond Diet

The Rotation Diet

The Low-Fat Good Food Cookbook
(with Terri Katahn)

How to Quit Smoking without Gaining Weight

Martin Katahn, Ph.D.

W·W·Norton & Company

New York   London

First published as a Norton paperback 1996

The text of this book is composed in Berkeley Old Style,
with the display set in Futura Medium Condensed
Composition and manufacturing by the Haddon Craftsmen, Inc.
Book design by Margaret M. Wagner

ISBN 0-393-31522-3 pbk.

Library of Congress Cataloging-in-Publication Data

Katahn, Martin.
        How to quit smoking without gaining weight / Martin Katahn.
            p.   cm.
        ISBN 0-393-03714-2
        1. Reducing diets. 2. Ex-smokers—Nutrition. 3. Smoking
cessation programs. 4. Reducing exercises. 5. Weight loss.
I. Title.
RM222.2.K3465   1994
616.86'506—dc20   94-34378
                                                        CIP

W. W. Norton & Company, Inc., 500 Fifth Avenue, New York, N.Y. 10110
W. W. Norton & Company Ltd., 10 Coptic Street, London WC1A 1 PU

1 2 3 4 5 6 7 8 9 0

CONTENTS

| Money-Back Guarantee | page 108 |

ACKNOWLEDGMENTS

I'd like to extend special thanks to Jacqueline Goffaux, Ph.D., of the Institute for Smoking Prevention and Cessation at the Dayani Human Performance Center of Vanderbilt University, for reading my manuscript and making many helpful comments and suggestions.

Thanks to Marlene McCrate Otto, M.S., R. D., for helping to compile the Fat and Carbohydrate Counter in Appendix C.

And, once again, many thanks to my agent, Richard Pine, and the team at W. W. Norton & Company that helped me put this book together: my editor, Starling Lawrence; manuscript editor, Debra Makay; production manager, Andy Marasia; editorial assistant, Patricia Chui; and managing editor, Nancy Palmquist.

ACKNOWLEDGMENTS

Introduction

Have you been thinking that it's time to quit smoking but keep putting it off because you're worried about gaining weight?

Or are you one of those persons who has already quit smoking cigarettes, gained weight, and found yourself graduated to a whole new wardrobe a full size or two larger than before?

How to Quit Smoking without Gaining Weight will help you quit smoking without gaining an ounce, and it will help you lose whatever weight you have gained if you have already quit. It is based on my fifteen years of professional experience as director of the Vanderbilt Weight Management Program, my own personal experience as a former pack-a-day cigarette smoker, and the most recent research on smoking cessation.

To begin with, your fears about gaining weight when you

quit smoking are well founded. About 70 percent of the people who quit gain weight. Among these persons, the average gain is between 10 and 12 pounds. About one in seven women and one in ten men will gain 30 pounds or more. Some people gain at the rate of a pound a week, or even faster. I have worked with people who ended up 50 pounds heavier less than a year after quitting.

But don't be discouraged by these statistics! I'm so certain that the advice on weight management in this book will work for you that I am making a **MONEY-BACK GUARANTEE** to anyone who gives my plan an honest try and still can't control his or her weight (see page 108 for details).

If you are still smoking cigarettes, you are most likely thinking seriously about quitting or you would not be reading this book. You may be concerned about your risk for lung cancer, emphysema, and heart disease, and, if you are a parent with children at home, the danger of passive smoke to their health. To quit smoking is about the very best thing you can do for your own health as well as for the health of the people around you.

Wouldn't it be a whole lot easier to quit and never be tempted to start again if you didn't have to worry about gaining weight? Although gaining a small amount of weight is not nearly as dangerous as smoking, the more you gain, the more you restore the risk of heart disease and certain forms of cancer that you reduced by quitting. Of course, adding more than a few pounds can result in a cosmetic disaster and a loss of self-esteem.

What's even worse about gaining weight after you quit smoking (and I really hate to say this since it is so important

to quit) is that IT IS MUCH HARDER TO LOSE A SIGNIFI-
CANT AMOUNT OF WEIGHT THAN IT IS TO QUIT
SMOKING! About half the adults in this country who once
smoked cigarettes have, usually after several attempts, been
able to quit smoking permanently. Fewer than one in ten
overweight persons is able to lose a significant amount of
weight and keep it off for good, no matter how many times
they try.[1]

WHY I DECIDED TO WRITE A BOOK ON HOW TO QUIT SMOKING WITHOUT GAINING WEIGHT

I decided that a book on how to quit smoking without gaining weight might be of value to a great many smokers and
ex-smokers when, one day in October 1993, my wife came
home after shopping for a gown to use while performing.[2]
She told me that the two salespersons who helped her at the
dress shop had recently quit smoking. One of the women
had gained 12 pounds, and was a whole dress size larger.
The other woman had gained 6 pounds and was on the
verge of bursting her seams. They were not very happy
about this and they both pleaded, "Your husband needs to
write a book on how to quit smoking without gaining
weight!"

By a strange coincidence, the very day that my wife came

[1]"Overweight" is usually defined as being 20 percent over the weight specified as
desirable in standard weight charts.
[2]Enid Katahn is professor of music at Vanderbilt University and a concert pianist.

home with this request I received a letter from a man who had gained weight after quitting smoking. Then he discovered *The T-Factor Diet* and with its help he lost all the weight he had gained, plus an additional 32 pounds that he had needed to lose before he quit smoking. Here is an excerpt from that letter, dated October 12, 1993:

> I am writing to say a hearty "thank you" for your book, *The T-Factor Diet.* I found it in September, 1991, after gaining ten pounds as a result of smoking cessation. Or, should I say my lack of control during that six week period after quitting.[3] I am walking testimony to the ongoing success of your program. From September, 1991 until May, 1992, I lost forty-two pounds. At this writing, my weight remains at the May, 1992 level, with very minor fluctuations. My range is now from 149 to 151.

My wife's experience at the dress shop, and the receipt of this letter, encouraged me to do some research in the field of smoking cessation. I had been asked in my lectures on weight management to give advice on how to quit smoking without gaining weight many times before, but had never responded by writing a book, or even an article, about it. Aren't people already given the information they need about the many factors that lead to weight gain when they quit smoking? Isn't the best information on how to prevent weight gain easily available from the major health organizations interested in helping people quit smoking?

[3]As you will discover when you understand the reasons for gaining weight when you quit smoking, this person had no need to blame a lack of control.

The answer is NO!

When I studied the manuals of the major health organizations I discovered that, in their eagerness to get you to stop smoking, they downplay both the likelihood of gaining weight when you quit and the amount that you are likely to gain. They also do not give a full explanation of the physiological and biochemical changes that may occur in your body when you withdraw from nicotine, *changes which are out of your control.* Furthermore, the advice on how to deal with these physiological changes and prevent gaining weight after you have quit smoking does not work for the great majority of quitters who end up gaining 10, 12, or even 50 pounds. The net result is that most quitters feel lousy about the weight they gain. And because they have been led to believe that gaining weight was going to be a minor problem or should not be happening in the first place, they feel guilty over their inability to prevent it.

In addition to studying the smoking-cessation manuals of the major health organizations, I did a computer-assisted search and found over 1100 articles in the scientific literature on the biochemical effects of nicotine, metabolism, smoking-cessation strategies, and the problem of weight gain, written within the past ten years. When I studied these articles, I discovered a number of factors that are specific to smokers and that cause smokers in particular to gain weight when they quit. These factors are not discussed in smoking-cessation manuals or, to my knowledge, in any books on weight management, including my own earlier books, *The T-Factor Diet* and *One Meal at a Time.*

That's why I decided to write this book.

In *How to Quit Smoking without Gaining Weight* I present two closely related programs.

The 7 + 7 Program is designed for persons who are about to quit. In this program I will show you, in two consecutive seven-day training periods, how to make sure, *in advance,* that you will not gain any weight when you quit smoking, and then how to choose the best way to do it.

For persons who have already quit and who, unfortunately, may have gained some weight, I present the Ex-Smoker's Weight-Management Program. This program will show you what you need to do to lose weight without endangering your ability to remain a non-smoker.

So, without further introduction, let's jump in and see where you stand and what you need to do to quit smoking without gaining weight.

HOW TO
QUIT SMOKING
WITHOUT GAINING
WEIGHT

1

WHAT DO YOU NEED TO KNOW?
WHAT DO YOU NEED TO DO?

Do you know why most smokers gain weight when they quit?

If you are about to quit, do you know what to do to fight successfully against the craving for a cigarette the moment it hits you?

Do you know your underlying reasons for smoking, and how to deal with them so that when you quit you won't keep yearning for cigarettes?

Here are a couple of quizzes to test your understanding of the problems that are reflected in the above questions, together with a brief explanation to go with the answers. In the chapters that follow, I will go into greater detail in order to give you the weapons you will need to become a non-smoker at the weight you'd like to be.

Quiz 1 · WHY DO YOU GAIN WEIGHT WHEN YOU QUIT SMOKING?

1. TRUE OR FALSE: When you quit smoking it's possible to gain weight even though you don't consume a single calorie more than you did as a smoker.

2. TRUE OR FALSE: There is a physiological basis to the increase in appetite that most people experience when they quit smoking, and it usually does lead them to eat more than they did before.

3. TRUE OR FALSE: There is a physiological basis to the craving for sweets that develops in many people who quit smoking.

4. TRUE OR FALSE: When smokers quit, their bodies may begin to convert more of the fat in their diets to body fat than when they were smokers.

5. TRUE OR FALSE: Smoking can increase your metabolic rate so that pack-a-day smokers may be able to eat as much as 200 calories more each day without gaining weight, compared with non-smokers.

Did you answer "true" to all the above questions? If you did, you are absolutely correct: You can gain weight when you quit smoking even if you don't eat a single calorie more than you did as a smoker. But, just to compound the problem, your appetite is also likely to increase, especially your appetite for sweets. In addition, when you withdraw from nicotine, your fat cells may start to suck up fat from your bloodstream after you have eaten at a faster rate than they did when you smoked. Finally, if you smoke about a pack of cigarettes a day and quit, your total daily energy needs may decline by as much as 200 calories. When you add the increased rate of fat storage to the decline in your energy requirements, it means that unless you do something to compensate for these changes, you may need to consume about 300 calories less each day just to maintain your present weight when you quit smoking.[1] And all at the same time that your appetite may be going berserk![2]

I will give you a full explanation of how and why these things occur in the next chapter, "Know Your Enemy." Then, whether you are about to quit or have quit already and gained some weight, you will understand why you must take the steps I recommend, and you will be more motivated to take them.

Now, about the smoking habit itself.

The next several paragraphs are intended primarily for smokers about to quit. However, if you have recently quit, you should still read them and answer the questions in the quiz just in case you are continuing to struggle with the urge to smoke.

---

[1]When they discuss the impact of smoking on your energy needs some experts prefer to use the term "total daily energy expenditure" rather than "metabolic rate," which usually refers to the rate at which your body burns calories at rest. The reason for this is, in part, that smoking may increase energy needs during physical activity even more than when you are at rest.

[2]There are a few studies in respected, peer-reviewed scientific journals that present evidence for each of these physiological changes in response to smoking cessation. If you are likely to gain a small amount of weight when you quit, it's virtually certain that at least one of these mechanisms will be operating. If you are a heavy smoker and have any genetic tendency to obesity, it's likely that several of these factors will combine to foster a large weight gain. Since it's impossible to predict which factors may operate in any particular case, an ounce of prevention is worth a pound of cure: You should be prepared to deal with all of them, *before you quit smoking.*

If you are still smoking cigarettes and are seriously considering quitting, you have to ask yourself:

AM I REALLY READY TO KICK THE SMOKING HABIT?
AM I CONFIDENT I CAN DO IT SUCCESSFULLY?

Two conditions are absolutely essential if you are going to be a successful quitter:

1. You must be highly motivated to quit.
2. You must be confident in your ability to do it.

It's possible to be motivated to quit, but to waver for a couple of reasons. Because quitting can be rather uncomfortable, and cigarettes have been fulfilling an important function in your life, it's natural to debate the pros and cons of giving them up. And since most people who try to quit fail in any given attempt and need to try several times before they are successful, it's natural to lack absolute confidence in your ability to succeed, especially if you have failed one or more times in the past. Thus, a lack of confidence can actually undermine your motivation.

In case you are wavering, or thinking of putting off your quit date, let me remind you of certain statistics about smoking and some immediate benefits of quitting. I hope these will convince you that NOW is the right time to carry through with your intentions.

If you continue to smoke cigarettes, here are the risks:

• You will be twelve times more likely to die from lung cancer.
• You will be ten times more likely to die from other lung diseases.

- You will be ten times more likely to die from cancer of the larynx.
- You will be six times more likely to die from cancer of the mouth.
- You will be twice as likely to die of heart disease.
- You will be twice as likely to die of a stroke.

Reflect for a moment: Wouldn't it be extremely important for you to increase your chances, from two to twelve times, of gaining many extra healthy, happy, pain-free years in place of the long-term suffering and thousands of dollars in medical expenses associated with this list of illnesses?

But you don't have to wait many years to be aware of the good you do yourself by quitting. There are some immediate benefits that you can find out for yourself by just asking any successful quitter how he or she feels. They will most likely tell you, as one recently told me, "It's an ego builder. You feel like a different person."

Now let's talk about self-confidence. How can you increase confidence in your ability to be successful?

First of all, you need to be able to answer this question:

What will you do to resist the desire to smoke each time it hits you, and will you be able to do it until the urge passes?

When the craving for a cigarette descends on you, you need some "short-range artillery" to shoot it down. I have the perfect weapons for you, and I'll show you how to use them in the 7 + 7 Program. With these weapons you *will* be able to resist the desire to smoke each time it hits you, and you *will* be able to do it until the urge passes.

Second, and more important in the long run, is that you

need to be able to deal with your underlying reasons for smoking. What kind of satisfaction—physical, mental, and emotional—has smoking been providing?

On the next page is a brief quiz to determine why you are (or formerly were) smoking cigarettes.

Each one of the questions in Quiz 2 reflects a different emphasis in your need for cigarettes. Usually, smokers rate questions in two or more of the different groups at the 3 or 4 level. If this applies to you, you will have to learn to cope with a number of different feelings and situations without the help of cigarettes.

A high rating on one or both of the questions in Group 1 suggests that you use cigarettes for stimulation or extra energy. For example, you may smoke to stay alert or for a boost while doing things that require concentration or extra effort of any kind. Cigarettes may help you stay awake when your body says it's time to sleep, but you have work to finish.

A high rating on one or both questions in Group 2 suggests that smoking adds to the pleasure of relaxing—physically, mentally, or both. You may use cigarettes during work breaks, after finishing a tough job, or when you settle back for a cup of coffee or alcoholic beverage.

A high rating on one or more questions in Group 3 suggests that smoking is used to help you deal with negative affect. Smoking makes you feel better when something causes you to be angry, tense, anxious, or depressed.

The questions in Group 4 reflect psychological dependency. You worry about being out of cigarettes before it happens and before you suffer any form of nicotine deprivation.

Quiz 2 · MY MOST IMPORTANT REASONS FOR SMOKING

Circle the appropriate number:

1 = Never
2 = Sometimes
3 = Frequently
4 = Always

1. a. I smoke when I need a pickup.   1 2 3 4
   b. I smoke to keep from slowing down.   1 2 3 4

2. a. I smoke for the pleasure of it.   1 2 3 4
   b. I like to light up when I am comfortable and
      relaxed.   1 2 3 4

3. a. I smoke when I'm angry.   1 2 3 4
   b. I smoke when I'm anxious.   1 2 3 4
   c. I smoke when I'm tense.   1 2 3 4
   d. I smoke when I'm depressed.   1 2 3 4

4. a. I get anxious when I think I might run out of
      cigarettes.   1 2 3 4
   b. I get anxious if I must go someplace where I
      will not be able to smoke when I really
      want to.   1 2 3 4

5. a. I smoke a cigarette within thirty minutes after I
      get up in the morning.   1 2 3 4
   b. I smoke when I'm not feeling well.   1 2 3 4
   c. I smoke a pack (or more) a day.   1 2 3 4

6. a. Sometimes I smoke just to keep my hands
      busy.   1 2 3 4
   b. I smoke when I am bored.   1 2 3 4

A high rating on questions in Group 5 suggests a chemical addiction. If you answered all three with a high rating, it means that without a periodic "hit" you soon begin to experience withdrawal symptoms and feel quite uncomfortable.

A high rating on the questions in Group 6 suggests that smoking is something to do with your hands when you are nervous or uncomfortable, perhaps in social situations, maybe in place of eating (!). Or you may light up simply as something to do when you are bored, when having nothing to do makes you fidgety.

The several different categories of questions in the above quiz show the great variety of different gratifications that smoking can provide to different people with different needs. Nicotine is a versatile and powerful drug! It is more addicting than heroin or cocaine. And cigarette manufacturers have recently been accused of manipulating the nicotine content of their cigarettes, adding nicotine if necessary to maintain a constant predetermined amount in each cigarette, so that once you choose your brand you will get the same dose of the drug each time you smoke![3] Is it any wonder that so many millions have become dependent on nicotine, and that it is so difficult to quit smoking?

I will give you a brief but thorough description of the mechanisms through which nicotine exerts its powerful effects in the next chapter. But right now, in advance, I want to assure you that whatever *your* main reasons for smoking, the

[3]A memo circulated internally at one of the major cigarette manufacturers contains the following: "Without nicotine . . . there would be no smoking. . . . Think of the cigarette as a dispenser for a unit dose of nicotine" (*Business Week,* March 14, 1994).

7 + 7 Program will give you a whole new set of strategies for obtaining satisfaction equal to or greater than the satisfaction you now obtain from nicotine, without any of the life-threatening dangers of smoking cigarettes.

2

KNOW YOUR ENEMY

What is it that makes cigarette smoking so addictive?

If you smoke more than a few cigarettes a day, why do you feel so lousy when you try to quit?

Why does your appetite increase when you quit smoking?

And how, for goodness' sake, even if you don't eat a single crumb more than before you quit smoking, is it *still* possible for you to gain weight?

Nicotine elicits some powerful biochemical reactions that have an almost instantaneous effect on your mood, your cognitive abilities, your appetite, and your metabolism. Since nicotine can result in pleasant feelings and its impact can actually be helpful in certain situations, it is easy to become physically and psychologically dependent on cigarettes.

Some smoking-cessation experts like to differentiate the degree of dependence on cigarettes into several levels, depending on how much and when you smoke. Of course, the more you smoke, the more your body adjusts its chemistry to high levels of nicotine intake, which can lead to a true chemical dependence. However, even light smokers can become just as dependent on cigarettes because of nicotine's psychological impact, that is, the way it affects their mood and their feelings in certain situations. This can lead to a strong psychological dependency specific to those situations, and can be independent of the actual amount smoked each day. It turns out that the severity of withdrawal symptoms when you quit can be just as severe as a result of psychological dependency among light to moderate smokers as it can be as a result of chemical dependency among heavy smokers. Finally, because of the complexity of factors involved, moderate smokers are likely to gain as much weight as, or even more than, heavy smokers when they quit.

I'm going to start by explaining how nicotine brings about the physiological and psychological reactions that contribute to your underlying reasons for smoking. You will then understand the physiological basis for the answers you gave to the quizzes in the previous chapter, and you will understand why you need to follow the 7 + 7 Program to compensate for these reactions when you quit smoking.

THE BIOCHEMICAL EFFECTS OF NICOTINE

It's only a matter of seconds before the impact of nicotine from the first puffs of a cigarette is felt in the central nervous system and throughout your body. There are nicotine receptors in several parts of the brain, one of which increases arousal when stimulated by nicotine and can help you think more clearly. Other receptors lie in a "pleasure" center of the brain, which, when stimulated by nicotine, can make you feel more relaxed and less anxious.

The impact of nicotine is very powerful because it affects many different neurotransmitters and hormones that were meant to help a person cope with dangers of all kinds. Levels of catecholamines (epinephrine, norepinephrine, and dopamine), beta-endorphins, and cortisol in the central nervous system and bloodstream increase with each puff of a cigarette. These substances are mobilized whenever a person is injured or stressed in any way, physically or mentally. Thus, when you smoke a cigarette, the biochemicals that are secreted can help you feel less tense and more able to cope with whatever is stressing you. It takes just one cigarette (or for some people, two) for these neurohormonal substances in your body to reach an effective level.

The impact of these hormones lasts a certain amount of time after you've finished your cigarette because they keep circulating in your bloodstream. However, after each cigarette, your body goes to work to eliminate the excess and return to its normal baseline levels. You can become addicted to or dependent on the physical and psychological effects of these naturally occurring chemicals in the body which are stimulated by nicotine just as you can to amphetamines, heroin, and other painkillers, which are chemically similar to epinephrine, norepinephrine, beta-endorphin, and cortisol.

There tends to be a difference in the physiological, or chemical, dependency on nicotine between light and heavy smokers. Light smokers tend to use cigarettes only when they feel the need for nicotine's psychological impact, for example, to help deal with stress while working on a particular problem or to relax after dealing with it. They may use a cigarette to help reduce the initial tension in social situations, such as when they arrive at a cocktail party, or because a cigarette enhances the pleasure associated with a cup of coffee or a martini. After a time, smoking can become a habit in these situations even when the psychological need is absent—you just automatically reach for a cigarette when you find yourself in a particular place doing a particular thing at a particular time.

Heavy smokers have become chemically dependent on heightened levels of hormones, stimulated by nicotine, which can have "addicting" qualities. They need a cigarette with a certain periodicity, starting within thirty minutes or so after they get up in the morning. Then, as the level of hormones stimulated by each cigarette falls, they need another "hit." It can be every twenty, thirty, or forty minutes, but if more than that period of time goes by, they begin to crave a cigarette.

Both light smokers, when denied the psychological support of nicotine in accustomed situations, and heavy smokers, when denied their periodic nicotine hit for even twenty-four hours, can begin to experience one or more characteristics of the withdrawal syndrome: anxiety, restlessness, irritability, cigarette cravings, inability to concentrate, dysphoria, hunger, and drowsiness followed by insomnia when they try to fall asleep at night. Is it any wonder it's hard to quit!

But why does cigarette smoking help to control your weight, and why do most people gain weight when they quit? Is it simply a lack of willpower or self-control?

WHY SMOKING CESSATION IS LIKELY TO LEAD TO WEIGHT GAIN

Unfortunately, cigarette smoking really is an aid to weight management. Here is how it works and why it is so effective.

Nicotine can reduce your desire to eat by directly affecting the activity of serotonin and dopamine, which are substances that control neural transmission in areas of your brain that turn your appetite on and off. Nicotine elevates the activity of these substances in a way that is somewhat similar to what happens when you eat a piece of candy; for a certain period after smoking a cigarette or eating that candy you feel less hungry.

Nicotine causes your adrenal glands to release catecholamines which in turn cause the liver to release glucose into the bloodstream and your fat cells to release fatty acids. This increases the energy available to all the cells of your body, and the reaction is similar to what happens after you eat, which also may help reduce your appetite.

The catecholamines are stimulants and they cause your metabolic rate to increase sharply within seconds after you begin smoking. The increase appears to be even greater during physical activity than when you are sitting still. If you smoke a pack or a pack and a half of cigarettes each day, your daily energy needs can be increased by about 200 calories. Some experts believe that a good part of this increase is due to the higher rate at which those fatty acids keep circulating in and out of your fat cells each time you smoke. That is, out come the fatty acids at the onset of smoking, and then back they go into the fat cells in between cigarettes. This work requires energy.

But there are a couple of even more insidious factors at work that can lead to weight gain when you quit smoking even though you don't eat an ounce more of anything. In fact, these factors can lead to weight gain even if you go on a reduced-calorie diet after you quit.

First, nicotine can cause an increase in the activity of the enzyme adipose tissue lipoprotein lipase (AT-LPL), which is responsible for incorporating fat into your fat cells. This appears to be a counterregulatory reaction and it's likely that the more you smoke, the greater the increase in this fat-storing enzyme. I want to explain this in more detail because, if you are one of those people who is likely to gain weight, I think it will add to your motivation to do what it takes to quit smoking without suffering that consequence.

Because nicotine increases metabolic rate and keeps pulling fatty acids from your fat cells and burning them up each time you smoke a cigarette, smoking can result in your being from 10 to 12 pounds, or even more, *below* the natural weight where you would be as a non-smoker. Your body tries to compensate for this nicotine-induced fat burning by working extra hard, increasing AT-LPL activity, to get what fat it can from your diet into your fat cells. The increased cycling of fatty acids in and out of your fat cells in between cigarettes may also stimulate heightened AT-LPL activity.

The extent of AT-LPL activity may be related to the amount smoked: The more you smoke, the greater the cycling, and the greater the AT-LPL activity.

When you stop smoking, the heightened activity of AT-LPL[1] can make fat incorporation much easier than if you had never been a smoker. Your hungry fat cells are just lying in wait to suck up the fat in your diet, in order to make up for the depletion that they have endured due to nicotine.

Second, besides the increased likelihood of gaining weight from the fat in your diet when you quit smoking, *recent research suggests that there may also be an increased likelihood of gaining weight from the carbohydrates you eat,* which does not occur for non-smokers. Because this research is so new, and because it may be especially important for heavy smokers who have a hereditary tendency to obesity, I want to go into some detail on this particular possibility.

Here is some background.

In order to be used or stored as energy, the carbohydrates that you eat are converted to glucose. The body stores only a small amount of glucose, about half in your muscle cells and the rest in your liver. In this way, whenever you need energy for moving around, some glucose is immediately available in the muscles themselves, and the glucose stored in the liver can be secreted into the bloodstream almost instantaneously to back up the muscles' supply. In any given day,

[1]How long this effect may last is not predictable in any given case. It may last weeks or months, and it may be responsible for just a few pounds of extra fat in one person and a great many pounds in another.

when you are at a stable weight, *almost none of the carbohydrate calories you eat is ever turned to fat for storage.* Daily fluctuations in carbohydrate intake are almost completely handled in the body by increasing and decreasing stores of glucose, not fat. *In order to gain fat weight from excess carbohydrate, you must continually outeat your energy needs by a considerable amount, day after day.* This holds true for both smokers and non-smokers.[2]

But here is the difference for smokers.

The hormone that controls the rate at which glucose is transported into the cells of your body is *insulin.* The more insulin circulating in your bloodstream, the faster glucose gets removed from your bloodstream and transported into your body cells. *The recent research I am talking about shows that smoking can depress insulin activity.* Thus, compared with non-smokers, the circulating levels of glucose in smokers will tend to be higher. Since the daily energy need of smokers is also higher, a good portion if not all of the extra glucose will be burned off and is not available either for storage in the muscles and liver or for conversion to fat.

When you quit smoking, *your circulating insulin level may go up,* which will make it easier for glucose to be transported into your muscles and liver. The immediate result is that

[2]Most people store between 2000 and 4000 calories in glucose, compared with 50,000 to 200,000, or even more, calories in fat. Glucose is stored in a ratio of 1 part glucose to 4 parts water, while fat is stored in a ratio of about 4 parts fat to 1 part water. It takes about 400 calories of glucose combined with water to add a pound of weight to your body, while it takes 3500 calories in fat plus water to add a pound of weight. But maximum storage of glucose can only add between 3 and 5 pounds to any person's weight. Then, if excess intake continues and is not burned off, it can become available for conversion to fat.

your muscles and liver will simply store more than their normal, pre-cessation levels of glucose. Because of the high volume of water that combines with glucose when it goes into storage, you can gain 3 to 5 pounds in a day or two.

At that point, however, your liver and muscles are stuffed to capacity. Where is excess glucose going to go if it can't get into your muscles and liver?

Excess glucose at that point becomes available for conversion to fat. And, in this connection, it becomes very important to remember that you may experience a decrease in total energy needs of up to 200 calories a day or even more when you quit smoking due to a decrease in your metabolic rate. Thus, if you continue your previous carbohydrate intake after you quit smoking, you will have an excess circulating amount of glucose in your bloodstream that has no place to go, except to be converted to fat and end up in your fat cells!

In other words, if, when you quit smoking, you eat just as you did before as a smoker, and don't find a way to burn up those surplus calories, including carbohydrate calories, you can first experience a quick gain in water weight and then *a portion of what was your customary carbohydrate intake can now end up as fat!*

So, talk about strikes against you! As a result of biochemical changes, when you quit smoking:

1. Your body's tendency to store dietary fat may go up.
2. Your body's tendency to store carbohydrates, either as glucose or as fat, may also go up.
3. Your total energy needs can go down about 200 calories a day.

4. And, if three strikes aren't enough, your appetite may increase, especially your taste for sweets! Here are the reasons for this phenomenon.

SMOKING CESSATION AND APPETITE

There are at least three reasons why quitters report an increase in appetite after quitting, with a particular increase in their desire for sweets.

First, one of the reasons you continue to smoke may be as a means of weight control, and you may reach for a cigarette just to have something in your hands and mouth other than food. It's a habit that may have developed to replace snacking when you take a break from work or when you first notice that you are just a little hungry in between meals, but not yet ready for lunch or dinner.

Second, if you tend to eat when you are nervous, and find that eating has a quieting, calming effect (which is a normal reaction, noted in most animals), you may have become accustomed to cigarettes for the same tension-reducing impact you would otherwise get from food. When you quit smoking, the desire to eat can now become overwhelming whenever you become tense.

Third, nicotine and carbohydrate foods, especially sweets, have a similar effect on serotonin activity in the brain. Thus, when you quit smoking, the substitution of a sweet can replace the biochemical impact of nicotine. This is a two-edged reaction: The eating of something sweet can help reduce the craving for a cigarette, *and it can help you be successful as a quitter.* The trick would be in finding a way to satisfy any sweet craving that occurs without adding to the difficulties you face in preventing weight gain.

Although studies show that appetite increases following smoking cessation, *the increase in caloric intake that occurs does not account for all the weight that is gained.* In quitters who gain weight, only about 70 percent of the gain is, on the average, due to increased food intake. People gain about 30 percent more weight than can be directly attributed to the added calories they have eaten. This unfortunate 30 percent "bonus" weight gain is due to the metabolic changes that occur after you quit smoking, of which the three most likely are the decrease in metabolic rate, the residual increase in AT-LPL activity, and the increase in the rate of glucose storage.

SO, WHAT TO DO?

I have gone into such detail about the impact of nicotine, especially on your weight, for several reasons. To begin with, you deserve a full explanation that does not downplay the problems associated with quitting. It's not as easy as it's made out to be, especially coping with your body's tendency to gain weight. There is no need to feel inferior or guilty because you somehow lack "willpower." When you consider the power of the drug:

IT'S NOT YOUR FAULT THAT YOU FEEL HUNGRY WHEN YOU QUIT.

IT'S NOT YOUR FAULT YOUR METABOLIC RATE DE-CREASES.

IT'S NOT YOUR FAULT THAT YOUR BODY RESPONDS

TO NICOTINE WITHDRAWAL WITH AN INCREASE IN INSULIN, AND YOU'VE ALSO GOT THAT RESIDUAL IN-CREASED AT-LPL ACTIVITY CAUSED BY SMOKING.

These are biological, not moral, issues! They are the usual, NORMAL reactions to nicotine use and to quitting.

However, my most important reason for going into such detail is that I believe you need to understand the rationale for each and every step that you must take to counter all of these physical and psychological effects. *How to Quit Smoking without Gaining Weight* will show you exactly what you need to do and what you are accomplishing when you do it. And this will increase and maintain your motivation to keep doing it.

We are now ready for the 7 + 7 Program for smokers who want to quit without gaining weight. *If you have already quit smoking, you must still read these two chapters.* They contain advice that will help you continue to be a successful non-smoker, as well as many nutritional suggestions that are as helpful for losing weight as they are for preventing weight gain when you quit. Study these next two chapters first, and then begin the Ex-Smoker's Weight-Management Program in Chapter 5.

The diet and activity program presented in *How to Quit Smoking without Gaining Weight* is safe for persons in good health. However, before changing your diet and starting an exercise program you should check with your physician to make sure the changes are suitable in your particular case. In addition, because nicotine interacts with a number of pre-scription and nonprescription drugs, magnifying or diminishing their impact, if you take any medication on a routine basis it is essential that you check with your physician before you quit smoking so that dosages of these interacting medications can be adjusted if necessary.

3

HOW TO QUIT SMOKING WITHOUT GAINING WEIGHT: THE 7 + 7 PROGRAM

PART 1: MANAGING YOUR WEIGHT

You can make sure you won't gain weight when you quit smoking by completing Part 1 of the 7 + 7 Program *before you quit.* (If you have already quit, you should still read this chapter and Chapter 4 before going on to the Ex-Smoker's Weight-Management Program since they contain important information for you as well as for smokers about to quit.)

Programs that have you quit smoking and *then* go on a diet to lose weight are self-defeating. Seeing yourself gaining weight while you are struggling to remain a non-smoker is stressful enough, but going on a diet to lose weight after you have quit smoking simply adds more stress to the stress already involved in smoking cessation. It's a fact: People who gain weight when they quit smoking and then try to adhere to a strict weight-loss diet *while they are still struggling to resist cigarettes* are more likely to relapse and start smoking again.

This will not happen to you when you use the 7 + 7 Program.

The 7 + 7 Program is a two-part program designed to be as stress-free as possible as you undertake the difficult job of stopping to smoke cigarettes. Each part normally takes seven days, but you can take longer if you feel the need for more practice, or you can jump ahead whenever you feel ready. You're the boss. My aim is to show you how to be in complete control and "stay cool" in situations where people who try to quit smoking feel frustrated and panic.

In Part 1 I will show you everything you need to do to prevent weight gain when you quit smoking. In Part 2 I will focus on smoking itself, and lead you through what research has shown to be the most effective approach to smoking cessation. If you have any doubts about your ability to kick the smoking habit, learning what you need to do to manage your weight *before* you quit will demonstrate that, given the right approach, you have the ability to change your behavior in some very significant ways. This demonstration will give you all the confidence you need to deal with cigarettes.

Your task in Part 1 of the program is to have all of your weapons *firmly in place* to combat a decrease in metabolic rate, an increase in the likelihood of fat and possibly carbohydrate storage, and a potential increase in your appetite, especially for sweets, one or all of which can occur when you quit smoking.

In the next seven days you will do this by:

1. Decreasing the fat in your diet while choosing the most healthful carbohydrate foods.

2. Starting an exercise program that will burn off any excess fat and carbohydrate in your diet that might otherwise be forced into storage by the heightened activity of AT-LPL that has occurred as a result of having smoked cigarettes and the increase in insulin that occurs upon quitting.

In addition, if you are a heavy smoker (a pack or more a day), I suggest you consult your physician sometime during this first week about nicotine replacement therapy, so that you will be ready to use either the patch or the gum when you quit smoking in Part 2. Nicotine replacement therapy can help minimize the metabolic changes that occur when you quit, as well as reduce withdrawal symptoms. Your physician will tell you how to use the patch and I will summarize instructions for nicotine gum in Part 2 to avoid any confusion about the use of the gum.

HOW TO CUT THE FAT IN YOUR DIET

Cutting the fat in your diet is THE most important nutritional change you can make, and it is quite easy when you use a one-meal-at-a-time approach. You simply take a look at what you customarily have been eating at each meal and as snacks, and make a few lower-fat substitutions. Making such substitutions serves a dual purpose. First, it prevents you from consuming any excess fat that your body can end up storing in your fat cells. Second, by reducing the amount of fat that's present in your meals, it forces your body to depend more upon the carbohydrate in your diet for energy throughout the day. This can prevent any increase in glucose storage that may occur as a result of heightened insulin activity in previously heavy smokers. In fact, if you follow all of the recommendations in the 7 + 7 Program, you will most likely be able to *increase* the amount of foods low in fat and higher in carbohydrates. This is desirable because a high-carbohydrate diet can help you fight the urge to smoke. If you choose the right foods, you will, in spite of eating more carbohydrates, still consume *fewer* total calories than before, since you will probably not be able to eat enough to equal your previous high-fat caloric intake.

Take a look at Tables 1 through 4. They contain tips and suggestions for making satisfying low-fat substitutions for high-fat foods for breakfast, lunch, dinner, and snacks. Then study my suggestions for low-fat meals on pages 60 through 64.

Table 1 · BREAKFAST SUGGESTIONS

SUBSTITUTIONS

In place of biscuits, croissants, doughnuts, pastries, or sweet rolls (12–20 g fat per serving), *substitute* whole-grain bread, raisin toast, English muffins, bagels, and bran or fruit muffins (1–3 g fat per serving).

In place of commercial muffins (10 g fat or more each), *make your own* from a recipe found on a bran flakes or other cereal box. Use low-fat milk, about half the fat called for, and egg substitute in place of whole eggs (3 g fat).

In place of whole milk (8 g fat per cup), *substitute* skim, ½ percent, or 1 percent milk (0–2 g per cup).

In place of butter or margarine (4 g fat per teaspoon), *substitute* jelly or jam (0 fat) or reduced-fat spreads (2–3 g fat per teaspoon).

In place of eggs (5 g fat each), *substitute* Egg Beaters (0 fat) or your favorite brand of egg substitute. When using eggs, boil or poach instead of frying or scrambling, which adds 4 g fat per teaspoon of fat.

In place of commercial sausage, regular style (5–10 g fat per ounce), *substitute* new low-fat versions (2 g fat per ounce).

In place of bacon (13 g fat per ¾ ounce, or 3 strips broiled crisp, cooked weight), *substitute* Canadian bacon or new reduced-fat versions (4 g fat per ¾ ounce, cooked weight).

TIPS

Use a variety of ready-to-eat cereals (1–3 g fat per serving). Mix a high-fiber variety with a favorite lower-fiber variety. Sweeten your cereal with fresh or dried fruit instead of sugar.

Flavor hot cereals with a touch of cinnamon or nutmeg, and add dried fruit.

Pancakes and French toast contain about 1 g fat each piece. Cook them in a pan with nonstick cooking spray or just enough fat to cover the bottom of the pan.

Top pancakes and French toast with powdered sugar, pancake syrup, fruit, or nonfat yogurt rather than butter or margarine (4 g fat per teaspoon).

Blend low-fat cottage cheese or yogurt cheese with salsa, onions, sardines, canned salmon, or various seasonings and use as a spread on English muffins, toast, or bagels. (Make yogurt cheese by allowing low-fat or nonfat yogurt to drip through cheesecloth or a coffee filter suspended over a bowl overnight.)

Use Grapenuts or Mueslix to add crunchiness to yogurt, hot cereals, or pancakes.

Use imitation bacon bits to add bacon flavor to eggs or Egg Beaters.

When eating out, ask your server to hold the butter or margarine on toast or pancakes. If you must, add a bit at the table. Use pancake syrup, jelly, or fruit in place of fat.

When eating out, ask to have your grits or cereal served without fat.

Table 2 · LUNCH SUGGESTIONS

SUBSTITUTIONS

In place of croissants (12–20 g fat), *substitute* whole-grain breads or rolls, bagels, or English muffins (1–2 g fat) for sandwiches.

In place of high-fat luncheon meats such as bologna or salami (6–8 g fat per ounce), *substitute* turkey, lean ham, or other lean luncheon meats (1–2 g fat per ounce).

In place of mayonnaise (11–12 g fat per tablespoon) on sandwiches, *substitute* low-fat mayonnaise or salad dressing (2–5 g fat per tablespoon) or, better, mustard or salsa (0 fat).

In place of high-fat dressings (7–9 g fat per tablespoon) for salads, *substitute* no- or low-fat dressings (0–2 g fat per tablespoon) or use only ½ tablespoon of a high-fat variety.

In place of cream- or cheese-based soups (10–15 g fat per cup), *substitute* broth-based soups, such as chicken noodle, minestrone, and vegetable (1–3 g fat per cup).

In place of potato or nacho chips (10 g fat per ounce) as accompaniments to sandwiches, *substitute* pretzels or breadsticks (1 g fat per ounce).

In place of high-fat snack crackers (4–6 g fat per ½ ounce), *substitute* low-fat crackers such as saltines, flatbread, melba toast, matzohs, or graham crackers (0–2 g fat per ½ ounce).

In place of regular cheese (8–10 g fat per ounce), *substitute* low-fat varieties (3–5 g fat per ounce) or, better yet, skip it altogether.

In place of high-fat cookies (4–6 g fat per serving) for brown-bag lunches, *substitute* fig bars, gingersnaps, animal crackers, graham crackers, cereal-marshmallow bars, or the new low-fat or nonfat varieties (0–2 g fat per serving).

TIPS

Cut up raw vegetables and store in water in an airtight container in the refrigerator. They will stay fresh and crisp for lunches, snacks, or cooking.

Keep a supply of canned tuna (water packed), salmon, sardines, clams, and crabmeat. Try them with different condiments, low-fat dressings, or as sandwich spreads.

Mix low-fat cottage cheese with dry soup mix, Cajun seasoning, salsa, clams, or any of your preferred herbs or seasonings for sandwich spreads and salads.

When visiting a salad bar, fill up on vegetables, garbanzo beans, and fruit. Use only small amounts of meats, cheese, eggs, and mayonnaise-based salads.

Table 3 · DINNER SUGGESTIONS

THREE WAYS TO LOWER THE FAT CONTENT OF YOUR REGULAR, FAVORITE RECIPES:

1. Substitute lower-fat ingredients.

2. Alter the basic method of preparation.

3. Reduce the amount of fat added.

FOR EXAMPLE:

1. Lean cuts of meat such as flank or round steak, *well-trimmed* sirloin, London broil, or pork tenderloin have only one-quarter to one-third the fat of ribeyes or chuck. If you don't trim well *before* cooking, the melted fat seeps between the lean muscle fibers and doubles the fat content of the cooked lean meat.

To tenderize lean meats, marinate for several hours with wine, soy sauce, or fruit juice (anything slightly acidic) and seasonings.

Choose extra-lean ground beef, ground round, or ground turkey (1–3 g fat per ounce, i.e., 90 percent lean or higher) rather than regular ground beef (10 g fat per ounce).

2. Use lower-fat preparation methods such as baking, roasting, broiling, grilling, poaching, steaming, or boiling rather than frying or cooking in fat. Frying can increase the fat content from two to six times, depending on the use of flour or batter.

3. Unless specifically designed as low-fat recipes, use only one-third to one-half of the fat called for.

**TIPS TO HELP YOU PUT THESE SUGGESTIONS
INTO PRACTICE:**

Flavor vegetables with herbs and seasonings rather than added fat. If you generally add meat fat to beans or vegetables, use an ounce or two of lean ham for meaty flavor.

Stock these low-fat kitchen essentials: nonstick vegetable spray, broth or stock, nonfat yogurt, canned evaporated skim milk, and an assortment of seasonings and spices.

Sauté vegetables in a nonstick skillet with cooking spray, broth, or wine rather than oil or butter.

When using shredded cheese (8–10 g fat per ¼ cup) in a recipe or casserole, use less of a stronger cheese like sharp cheddar, or use a reduced-fat variety (4–5 g fat per ¼ cup).

Blend low-fat cottage cheese with a touch of lemon juice for a creamy baked potato topping, or try a reduced-fat sour cream.

Substitute canned evaporated skim milk or skim milk with nonfat dry milk added for recipes that call for cream or whole milk.

Plan a meatless meal one or two nights a week. Try legumes and rice or pasta with a vegetable sauce.

Oven-fry instead of frying in fat—spray a baking dish with vegetable spray and bake at a high temperature, turning at least once. Dip fish or chicken in low-fat milk or egg whites and coat with seasoned bread crumbs.

When a recipe calls for canned cream soup, substitute at least one can with an equal volume of evaporated skim milk with cornstarch or flour added as a thickener.

Basic everyday, low-fat desserts include fresh fruit, angel food cake, low-fat cookies, low-fat puddings, frozen yogurt, ice milk, and sherbet.

Table 4 · SNACK SUGGESTIONS

SUBSTITUTIONS

In place of chocolate candy (13–14 g fat per serving), *substitute* Life Savers, jelly beans, gumdrops, or lemon drops (0 fat).

In place of potato chips, cheese snacks, and nacho crackers (10–14 g fat per serving), *substitute* pretzels, pita chips, rice cakes, bagels, or flatbread (0–1 g fat per serving).

In place of regular and premium ice cream (12–20 g fat per serving), *substitute* nonfat and low-fat frozen yogurt (0–3 g fat per serving).

In place of nuts, including peanuts (10–14 g fat per serving), *substitute* popcorn (with oil) or Cracker Jacks (2 g fat per serving).

In place of chocolate-chip or other fatty cookies (4–6 g fat each), *substitute* gingersnaps, fig bars, or nonfat cookies (0–1 g fat each).

In place of croissants or butter rolls (10–20 g fat each), *substitute* whole-grain rolls, pita bread, or bagels (1–4 g fat each).

In place of Danish, doughnuts, pies, or frosted cakes (10–20 g fat each), *substitute* raisin bread and rolls, angel food cake, and fudge sauce (1–3 g fat).

TIPS

Fresh and dried fruit are your best sweet snacks and should be your first choices for sweets.

Vegetables such as carrot and celery sticks, sweet peppers, and summer squash are good, crunchy choices.

ESPECIALLY FOR SMOKERS

In place of smoking a cigarette, suck ONE piece of hard candy or chew gum. If eating one piece of candy turns on your appetite for sweets, eat instead a piece of fruit or a serving of crackers, such as Ryekrisp, Wasa bread, Ryvita, or melba toast, as your in-between-meal snack.

Many people who quit smoking find that the instructions I've just given are all they need to put an effective program into practice. If you hate to keep records of everything you eat and can make the changes I've just suggested without writing everything down, this informal approach may work for you. You are ready to begin! Just follow my recommendations in the food tables and, in addition, look up the fat content of the foods you normally eat as you go through the next seven days so that you can make specific low-fat substitutions for these foods. Use the Fat and Carbohydrate Counter in Appendix C. In place of high-fat versions, choose low-fat dairy products, lean cuts of meat, low-fat desserts and snacks, and plenty of fruit, vegetables, and grain products. If, at the end of seven days, you have made satisfying substitutes at all your meals and for snacks, and are following my suggestions for physical activity below, you will be ready to go on to Part 2 in the next chapter. However:

Would you like a guarantee that your approach will work?

You can *guarantee* that you are making the changes in your diet that will enable you to quit smoking without gaining weight by becoming a little more scientific. But before showing you how to do this, I need to review some nutritional guidelines and explain why you need to think in terms of grams of fat in your diet to implement these guidelines, rather than percentages.

If you are like a majority of Americans, your present diet contains more fat than is good for you whether you smoke or not. Health authorities without exception recommend that you obtain no more than 30 percent of your calories from fat, while a majority recommend that you decrease to 20 or 25 percent.[1] Between 60 and 65 percent of your calories should be obtained from carbohydrate, and about 10 to 15 percent from protein. But very few people need to be concerned about their intake of carbohydrate or protein when they reduce their fat calories. When you cut the fat content of your diet, and substitute the high-carbohydrate foods that I recommend, carbohydrate and protein percentages take care of themselves without any special attention or further calculations.

As a practical matter, it is much simpler to set a target for fat consumption each day in terms of total grams rather than beat your brains out trying to average the percentage of fat from a day's eating from foods that contain different percentages based on a different number of calories. For example, try calculating the percentage of fat for the following healthful dinner, averaged across the three dishes:

Baked sole with a teaspoon of butter and a squeeze of lemon: 202 calories, 37 percent fat

[1]If you already suffer from cardiovascular disease, you might do even better reducing your intake of fat to as low as 10 percent. However, this drastic a change in your diet should be discussed first with your physician.

Medium baked potato with a teaspoon of butter: 238 calories, 16 percent fat

½ cup steamed broccoli: 46 calories, 8 percent fat

Quick: What's the percent fat content of this meal?

Can you imagine trying to figure this out for an entire day, day after day?

It is far easier to think in terms of grams of fat per day than it is to average percentages. For example, if you are a woman who can maintain her weight by eating around 1600 calories per day, a target of 25 percent fat would be 44 grams. By looking up the fat content in the Fat and Carbohydrate Counter in Appendix C, you would quickly discover that the above meal contains 11 grams of fat. You would have 33 to go to meet your daily target of 44 grams. Other than simply adding the grams of fat in each dish, no complicated mathematical operations are required.[2]

Under normal circumstances, if you were not under the gun with respect to fat intake during the process of smoking cessation, you would choose a target for daily fat intake from Table 5, which contains the amount of fat in grams for different percentages of total calories. A woman who can maintain desirable weight on 1800 calories and who wishes to choose a healthful target of 25 percent of calories from fat would set an upper limit of 50 grams per day; a man on a diet of 2200 calories would aim for 61 grams.

However, as a person about to quit smoking, you have a special problem. You must compensate for a possible metabolic slowdown that can equal as much as 200 calories per

[2]This illustrative meal contains 486 calories, of which 99 are obtained from fat (11 grams of fat × 9 calories per gram = 99 calories). Thus, about 20 percent of the calories in the meal come from fat.

day (or more in heavy smokers), plus a possible tendency on the part of your fat cells to suck up fat from your diet to the tune of about another 100 calories a day. In other words, we must find a way to eliminate or burn up about 300 calories a day to prevent you from gaining weight.

Our two primary weapons are cutting the fat in the diet and increasing physical activity. I suggest you aim to consume at least 20 grams of fat less per day than you are doing now. That will equal about 180 fewer calories in fat available for storage. If cutting 20 grams of fat from your present diet leaves you consuming more than 25 percent of calories from fat, cut more. It is even better to reduce fat consumption to 20 percent of calories, but under no conditions should a woman cut below 20 grams of fat a day or a man 30 grams without a medical reason and the supervision of a qualified health professional. Your body needs a small amount of fat in your diet in order to carry out basic metabolic functions.

What about carbohydrate?

Excess carbohydrate is not likely to become a problem for most people who quit smoking when they follow the preceding instructions for reducing fat consumption. However, in order to be sure that you won't gain weight, you must monitor your intake of carbohydrate as well as fat, at least until such time as you determine that your consumption is not going to cause you any difficulty.

As I explained previously, some smokers may experience a difficulty with carbohydrate consumption because of an increase in insulin activity as a result of quitting. This in turn may result in a temporary increase in the amount of glucose that is stored in your muscles and liver. This is really water weight and, while it may temporarily amount to several pounds, this weight is not likely to end up as fat weight. Unless you outeat your total daily energy needs by a considerable amount, day after day, almost no carbohydrate in your diet is converted to fat for storage. So focus on decreasing your fat intake and making sure your carbohydrate intake does not continually exceed your daily energy needs, and you will see no permanent weight gain. Of course, you can add an additional guarantee that your carbohydrate intake will not exceed your energy needs by following my recommendations for physical activity, which, by the way, will also help prevent excess water retention.

The real problem with carbohydrate is likely to occur only for people who develop a craving for sweets when they quit smoking. While many quitters find that a piece of hard candy, such as a Life Saver, is an excellent way to fend off the immediate desire for a cigarette, some people lose control of themselves and begin to eat anything in which the calories come entirely from sugar. Instead of finding that one piece satisfies, once they start, they can't stop until they finish a whole package.

In part this reaction may also be related to changes in insulin activity. It occurs because these persons experience what's called an "insulin overshoot." Their bodies react to sugar by secreting more insulin than is actually required to maintain normal levels of glucose in their bloodstream. Soon after consuming anything in which all the calories come from sugar, such as the hard candies which might otherwise be useful, the excess insulin reduces their blood sugar below normal, they become temporarily hypoglycemic, and they begin to crave more sugar just to return to normal. It becomes a vicious cycle.

If you already know from past experience that it's hard to contain your desire for sweets once you start to eat them, or if it begins to happen to you when you experiment with sucking a piece of hard candy in place of a cigarette, you must avoid straight sugar candies or sugar-sweetened gum. Instead, you should maintain a normal blood sugar level by eating a healthful three meals a day and snacking three times a day on complex-carbohydrate foods. Because complex carbohydrates are more slowly converted to glucose, they are not as likely to cause an insulin overshoot and the cyclic reaction that leads to increased sugar consumption. My best recommendations for snacks are listed in Table 4.

HOW TO SET A TARGET FOR FAT AND CARBOHYDRATE CONSUMPTION IN ORDER TO QUIT SMOKING WITHOUT GAINING WEIGHT

Step 1. For the first two of the next seven days, keep a record of your fat and carbohydrate intake in grams, together with total calories, *without making any changes* in your diet. Use the Fat and Carbohydrate Counter in Appendix C and keep this record as part of the Seven-Day Eating Record at the end of this chapter.[3]

[3]You can photocopy this Seven-Day Eating Record to use the next week and as long as you like. You will also find a Fourteen-Day Eating Record in Chapter 5 which will carry you through the next two weeks, after you have quit smoking.

Step 2. Starting on Day 3, use Table 5 to set a fat goal in grams that is between 20 and 25 percent of your average total calories, or at least 20 grams below your baseline of the previous two days, whichever is lower. (*Remember, do not go below 20 grams of fat per day if you are a woman or 30 grams if you are a man.*)

Set your daily target for carbohydrate, tentatively, at the average of your two-day baseline level, with the following flexibility in mind: If you cut 20 grams or more of fat from your diet, you may be able to add some carbohydrate. You

Table 5 · FAT-GRAM TOTALS FOR DIFFERENT PERCENTAGES OF TOTAL CALORIES

| Total Calories | Grams of Total Fat as a Percentage of Total Calories | | |
	20%	25%	30%
1200	27	33	40
1300	29	36	43
1400	31	39	47
1500	33	42	50
1600	36	44	53
1700	38	47	57
1800	40	50	60
1900	42	53	63
2000	44	56	67
2100	47	58	70
2200	49	61	73
2300	51	64	77
2400	53	67	80
2500	56	69	83
2600	58	72	87
2700	60	75	90

will know in a couple of days whether you can do this, since by cutting the fat while you are still smoking, you may begin to lose weight.

If you find that you can add some carbohydrate to your diet at this time, begin to do it as snacks. When you quit smoking, snacking on carbohydrate foods throughout the day can help allay the craving for cigarettes.

By following my recommendations for physical activity, which can make sure that you do not outeat your daily energy needs, you may find, as most people do, that you can actually add as many carbohydrate grams back to your diet as you have cut in fat, or even more, since carbohydrate contains only 4 calories per gram, whereas fat contains 9 calories per gram. Replacing fat with carbohydrate in your diet, in the form of fruit, vegetables, and grains, is basically desirable if you have been eating the typical American high-fat diet, since it will help you reach nutritional guidelines of 60 to 65 percent of total calories from carbohydrate. You can refer to Table 6 to determine the amount of carbohydrate in grams for different percentages of total calories.

Now, what about those total calories?

Recall that you may need to compensate for a total of 300 calories in metabolic slowdown and increased fat incorporation when you quit smoking. By adding 300 calories of physical activity to your daily regimen you may be able to come out even—no decrease in total caloric intake and still no weight gain. However, I suggest you start with a balanced fifty-fifty combination: Compensate in part on the energy-intake side by reducing total fat without a complete match-

Table 6 · CARBOHYDRATE-GRAM TOTALS FOR DIFFERENT PERCENTAGES OF TOTAL CALORIES

Total Calories	Grams of Total Carbohydrate as a Percentage of Total Calories		
	55%	60%	65%
1200	165	180	195
1300	179	195	211
1400	193	210	228
1500	206	225	244
1600	220	240	260
1700	234	255	276
1800	248	270	293
1900	261	285	309
2000	275	300	358
2100	289	315	341
2200	303	330	358
2300	316	345	374
2400	330	360	390
2500	344	375	406
2600	359	390	423
2700	371	405	439

ing increase in carbohydrate, and on the energy-output side, increase physical activity. When you reach the final goal in physical activity, as discussed later in this chapter, you may indeed find you can increase calories back to your baseline level.

Step 3. Starting on Day 3 and for the next five days, before you begin Part 2 of the program, begin to make low-fat substitutions at each meal and at snack times, according to the suggestions in Tables 1 through 4. Keep a record of your fat and carbohydrate intake, making sure you do not exceed your daily targets.

Here are some sample meals for breakfast, lunch, and dinner. (My snack suggestions appear in Table 4.) Suggestions highlighted in bold type refer to recipes in Chapter 6. The recipes contain additional nutritional information.

BASIC BREAKFASTS[4]

BREAKFAST 1

Orange, grapefruit, or tomato juice (0 fat)
Ready-to-eat cereal with sliced fruit (1–3 g fat)
Low-fat or skim milk (0–2 g fat per cup)
Slice of whole-grain toast (1 g fat; jelly optional, 0 fat)
Beverage (1 g fat for 1 teaspoon half-and-half)

BREAKFAST 2

Melon or other fresh fruit (0 fat)
Bagel, English muffin, or 2 slices toast (1–2 g fat)
Jam or jelly optional (0 fat)
Low-fat or skim milk (0–2 g fat per cup) OR
Beverage of your choice (1 g fat for 1 teaspoon half-and-half)

[4] I have included estimates only for fat content in these suggested meals since that is the most important nutrient over which you must exercise control. The carbohydrate content can vary to a certain degree in each of these meals, depending on your selection when I give several options and on the quantity, so you must look up the carbohydrate content for the foods you eat to be accurate.

Breakfast 3

Fruit or juice (0 fat)
Honey Bran Muffin (1 g fat) or 2 slices of raisin bread (2 g fat)
Jam or jelly optional (0 fat)
Beverage (1 g fat for 1 teaspoon half-and-half)

Breakfast 4

Fruit or juice (0 fat)
Hot cereal with cinnamon and raisins (2–4 g fat)
Toast (1 g fat per slice; jam optional, 0 fat)
Beverage (1 g fat for 1 teaspoon half-and-half)

Special Breakfast 5

Choice of fruit (0 fat)
French toast or pancakes (2 pieces or pancakes, 1–2 g fat per
    piece)[5]
Jam, jelly, or pancake syrup (0 fat)
Canadian bacon (1-ounce piece, 2 g fat)
Beverage (1 g fat for 1 teaspoon half-and-half)

BASIC LUNCHES

Lunch 1

Broth-based soup (1 g fat per cup)
Sandwich with 1 ounce sliced turkey, lean ham, or low-fat refried
    bean spread (3 g fat; 0 fat for mustard or ketchup; 2 g fat for 1
    tablespoon low-fat mayonnaise)

[5]Use frozen egg substitute for French toast, and recipe on the box of mix for
pancakes, and just enough fat to cover the bottom of your frying pan or griddle.

Fruit or raw vegetables (0 fat)
Beverage (1 g fat for 1 teaspoon half-and-half)

LUNCH 2

Tuna or chicken salad (3½ ounces, made with 1 tablespoon
   low-fat mayonnaise, 4 g fat)
Lettuce, assorted greens, fresh vegetables (0 fat)
Whole-wheat crackers (2–4 g fat)
Choice of fruit (0 fat)
Beverage (1 g fat for 1 teaspoon half-and-half)

LUNCH 3

Nonfat or low-fat yogurt with berries, banana, or other favorite
   fruit, mixed in blender (0–2 g fat)
Assorted raw vegetables (0 fat)
Whole-wheat crackers or pretzel sticks (2–4 g fat)
Beverage (1 g fat for 1 teaspoon half-and-half)

LUNCH 4

Baked potato served with ½ cup low-fat cottage cheese
(2–4 g fat)
Diced green onions and Cajun seasoning (optional, 0 fat)
Tossed salad with low-fat dressing (2 g fat)
Fruit (0 g fat)
Beverage (1 g fat for 1 teaspoon half-and-half)

LUNCH 5

Sardine sandwich (2 slices pumpernickel bread, 2 ounces canned
   sardines, drained, plenty of your favorite mustard, slice of
   tomato or romaine, a few bean sprouts, 9 g fat)
Beverage (1 g fat for 1 teaspoon half-and-half)

BASIC DINNERS

DINNER 1

Pasta with **Red Clam Sauce** (5 g fat)
Tossed salad with low-cal dressing (3 g fat)
Slice of Italian bread (1 g fat)
Seasonal fruit (0 fat)
Chocolate-Chip Cookie (5 g fat)

DINNER 2

Baked Bass with Lemon-Wine Bouillon (7 g fat)
Baked acorn squash (½ squash, 0 fat; with 1 teaspoon butter,
    4 g fat)
Brussels sprouts or other green vegetable (0 fat)
Low-fat frozen yogurt (3 g fat)

DINNER 3

Marinated Flank Steak (10 g fat)
Baked potato (0 fat)
Green beans with water chestnuts (0 fat)
Tossed salad with low-fat dressing (2 g fat)
Slice of whole-grain bread (1 g fat)
Citrus fruit cup (0 fat)

DINNER 4

Chicken Cacciatore (with 1 cup spaghetti, 5 g fat)
Broccoli or other green vegetable (your favorite way, 4 g fat for 1
    teaspoon butter)
Tossed salad with low-fat dressing (2 g fat)
Thick slice of French or Italian bread (2 g fat)
Angel food cake with berries (0 fat)

DINNER 5

Vegetarian Chili Texas Style (1 g fat)
Brown or wild rice (½ cup, 1 g fat)
Asparagus or other green vegetable (4 g fat for 1 teaspoon
    butter)
Slice of corn or rye bread (1 g fat)
Frozen low-fat yogurt (1–2 g fat per ½ cup)

THE 7 + 7 ACTIVITY PROGRAM

Previously sedentary people who included physical activity as part of their program to quit smoking will tell you without exception that becoming active played a key role in their success. There are many reasons for this.

- When people become physically active, they also become more self-confident and like themselves better. The feeling of increased competence is pervasive and affects every aspect of their lives, including their ability to quit smoking.
- When people get active they feel more energetic, and, specifically, they feel more capable of dealing with tension in their lives, without reliance on cigarettes.
- When people get active the smell of cigarette smoke often becomes offensive. Several months after quitting, ex-smokers who exercise daily will tell you that their bodies react somewhat violently if they inhale a cigarette or even sit next to a person who is smoking one.
- Finally, physical activity provides *the ultimate guarantee* that you won't gain weight when you quit smoking because it burns off the calories that were formerly burned off by smoking.

YOUR PHYSICAL ACTIVITY GOAL

On the average, a pack of cigarettes per day increases your daily energy needs to maintain your weight by about 200 calories.

Forty-five minutes of moving about in place of sitting still will also increase your daily energy needs by about 200 calories.

I think you get the picture.

So the real question is how to become motivated to get active *and stay that way*. It's one thing to begin an activity program. It's quite another to begin to think of yourself as "an active person." About 90 percent of the people who begin an activity program with periodic visits to a fitness center or any other "three-times-per-week" approach, as though it were a doctor's prescription, give up exercising within a year. For people who think of themselves as physically active persons, physical activity is part of their self-concept, and essential to the good feelings they have about themselves. Perhaps this comparison will make my meaning clearer: It's one thing to say "I play tennis three times a week," for the worthy purpose of staying slim and healthier, but quite another to say, "I am a tennis player."

The easiest way to become an active person, and to begin to think of yourself as an active person as part of your self-concept, is to build some kind of physical activity into your daily life. Begin by setting aside ten minutes *every day* for physical activity, and gradually increase the time to forty-five minutes, or more if your schedule permits. For example, go out from your home or workplace for a walk. Do it every day at the same time, if you can. At the end of about two weeks your walk will begin to feel like an essential part of your life. You will feel uncomfortable if you miss it, just as you do if you fail to brush your teeth at the customary time!

The occasional approach to activity, such as three times a week at the health club or participation in an occasional aerobics dance class, is certainly good for you, but by itself this approach will not become habitual and it will not lead to the fundamental change in the way you think about yourself that I am talking about. It takes doing something active *every day*. Of course, you can mix your activities. Take up an active sport, such as tennis, and alternate it with swimming, bicycling, or gentle jogging (if you are not overweight and your physician does not object for medical reasons). Rotate among these different activities from day to day, but you must be regular.

To experience the full psychological benefits of exercise it takes being active in one continuous period of about forty-five minutes in some fairly vigorous activity. However, if your schedule doesn't permit this, you can still end up burning all the calories you need to burn to compensate for those that previously went up in smoke by just getting up out of your chair for five minutes every hour and moving about as briskly as your environment permits. Pace the halls, climb a few flights of stairs, lift some light weights. Take every opportunity to increase the time your body is in motion. Every little bit helps. For example, make all appointments in other people's offices rather than your own, park as far as possible from any destination to which you drive and walk the remaining distance, choose a restaurant for lunch that requires a five- or ten-minute walk in each direction. Remind yourself that every five minutes of movement will burn about 25 calories. Even though this approach may not lead to a fundamental change in your self-concept, you will probably feel so much more energetic when you move about this way that it will become a part of your daily routine.

Table 7 contains the caloric energy expenditures for many different forms of physical activity. Aim to add physical activity requiring between 200 and 300 calories a day in energy expenditure to the movement that is otherwise required of you in your daily responsibilities.

If you choose walking as your main way to increase physical activity, one way to stay motivated is to buy a pedometer at your local sporting goods store and keep track of your total mileage each day. If you work in a sedentary occupation, you probably total about 2 miles a day. To maintain your weight, and help stay in excellent health, you need to average at least 5 miles a day. (On days when you substitute some other activity for walking, the caloric expenditure will be approximately the same, minute for minute, as long as these other activities involve your whole body, such as swimming or cycling, and they are done at about the same intensity as your walk.)

Whenever you feel the urge to smoke after you have quit, get up and move around or lift some light weights instead. Brief physical activity not only reduces the urge to smoke, it can give you the lift you might otherwise have obtained from nicotine.

Table 7 · APPROXIMATE ENERGY COSTS IN EACH 15 MINUTES OF VARIOUS ACTIVITIES*

Activity	Calories per 15 Minutes
Aerobic dancing	105
Badminton	99
Ballroom dancing, continuous	53
Basketball	141
Canoeing (recreational)	45
Cleaning house (steady movement)	63
Climbing hills (steady pace)	123
Cooking dinner	47
Cycling	
5.5 mph, level ground	66
9.4 mph, level ground	102
Football	135
Gardening (raking)	56
Golf (walking—no cart)	87
Gymnastics	88
Horseback riding	
walking	42
trotting (English style)	113
Judo	199
Piano playing	41
Rowing (machine, fast pace)	105
Running	
11 min. 30 sec. per mile	138
10 min. per mile	174
9 min. per mile	197
8 min. per mile	213
7 min. per mile	234
6 min. per mile	260
Skiing	
cross–country, walking pace	146
downhill	101

*Energy costs are calculated for persons weighing 150 pounds. For each 10 pounds more or less than 150 pounds, add or subtract 7 percent, respectively, from these figures.

Table 7 · (CONTINUED)

Activity	Calories per 15 Minutes
Squash	216
Swimming	
freestyle, moderate pace	143
sidestroke	125
Table tennis	69
Tennis	111
Typing (electric typewriter)	27
Volleyball	51
Walking	
3 mph, level ground	66
4 mph, level ground	99
downstairs, steady pace	50
upstairs, slow steady pace	151

THE IMPORTANCE OF STRENGTH TRAINING

Recent research has shown that anaerobic activities, such as light strength training, in combination with an aerobic activity, such as walking, can play a significant role in a smoking-cessation program and help prevent weight gain.[6] When you walk at a steady, moderate pace you burn relatively

[6]By definition, aerobic activities are done in the presence of oxygen. That is, your intake of oxygen keeps up with the need for oxygen. For example, when you walk at a moderate pace, you don't get out of breath and keep on breathing hard when you stop to make up for the oxygen deficit that occurs when you exercise more intensely. Anaerobic activities, such as lifting weights, use oxygen and the store of glucose in your muscles faster than they can be replaced—you go into oxygen deficit, you must take a rest and replenish the glucose in your muscles from the supply in your liver before you can repeat the activity, and you keep breathing harder for a time after you finish exertion.

more fat than glucose in your fuel mixture. When you engage in strength training you burn relatively more glucose than fat. Between the two forms of activity you help normalize the circulating levels of both fat and glucose in your bloodstream. Furthermore, by replacing a few pounds of fat tissue with muscle tissue, which is the usual consequence of exercise of both kinds but maximized with strength training, you increase your metabolic rate by a couple of percentage points around the clock. That's because, compared with fat cells, muscle cells are much more active and burn more calories even when you are sitting still or sleeping.

I suggest you purchase a set of light weights—3 pounds each for a woman and either 5 pounds or 3 kilos (6.6 pounds) each for a man—and begin the light strength-training program in Appendix A (or simply follow the suggestions that come with the weights). Aim for ten minutes a day. In addition, keep the weights handy so that whenever you feel the urge to smoke you can use them for a few moments instead of lighting up a cigarette. I strongly encourage you to try this since you may find, like many others, that lifting light weights for three to five minutes completely eliminates your desire to smoke and leaves you with a much more invigorated and satisfying feeling than you used to get from smoking a cigarette.

Keep a Daily Record

Be sure you are meeting a daily activity goal of a minimum of forty-five minutes of extra aerobic physical activity, plus ten minutes of strength training, by keeping a Daily Activity

Record. Use the form at the end of the chapter or devise your own. Keep an activity record, as well as an eating record, for at least three weeks after you quit smoking.

Now we are ready to go on to Part 2 of the 7 + 7 Program and do away with cigarettes.

SEVEN-DAY EATING RECORD

Column headings: FAT = FAT; CARB = CARBOHYDRATE; CAL = CALORIES. List the food you eat at all meals and for snacks. Look up the fat and carbohydrate grams, and the calories, in the Fat and Carbohydrate Counter in Appendix C. Keep this

	Day 1			Day 2			Day 3		
DATE BEGUN:	FAT	CARB	CAL	FAT	CARB	CAL	FAT	CARB	CAL
BREAKFAST									
SNACK									
LUNCH									
SNACK									
DINNER									
SNACK									
TOTAL									

record for the next seven days. You may photocopy it to use thereafter, or use the Fourteen-Day Eating Record in Chapter 5. Continue to monitor your food consumption after you quit smoking for at least three weeks.

Day 4			Day 5			Day 6			Day 7		
FAT	CARB	CAL	FAT	CARB	CAL	FAT	CARB	CAL	FAT	CARB	CAL

SEVEN-DAY ACTIVITY RECORD

List all of your extra daily aerobic and strength-training activities, with starting and ending times. Aim for at least forty-five minutes of aerobic activity, such as walking or its equivalent, and a minimum of ten minutes of light strength training. Make photocopies and keep this record for at least three weeks after you quit smoking.

DATE BEGUN:	ACTIVITY	START TIME	END TIME
DAY 1			
DAY 2			
DAY 3			
DAY 4			
DAY 5			
DAY 6			
DAY 7			

4

How to Quit Smoking without Gaining Weight: The 7 + 7 Program

PART 2: HOW TO BECOME A NON-SMOKER IN JUST SEVEN DAYS

When you complete Part 1 of the 7 + 7 Program you will be doing exactly what it takes to prevent gaining weight when you quit smoking. You will also have proved that you can make some significant changes in your life and become more like the person you want to be.

You are now ready to consider the question:

How and when do you want to quit smoking?

There are basically two ways to quit: immediately, "cold turkey," or gradually. To quit gradually you use various methods to taper off before smoking your last cigarette. Neither way has proven to be best for everyone. So you should choose the way that is most suited to your personal style and temperament. No matter which way you choose, nicotine gum or the patch can be a great help, especially if you are a heavy smoker.

Here is a little test to see which approach to quitting is likely to be best for you.

Quiz 3 · CHOOSING THE BEST QUITTING METHOD

Answer the following questions by circling "yes," "no," or "not sure."

1. Giving up smoking is one of the most important things in the world to me right now.   yes   no   not sure

2. I know how to handle tense situations without reaching for a cigarette.   yes   no   not sure

3. I know I need to quit smoking and my reasons for quitting are strong enough for me to do it right now, this minute.

yes   no   not sure

4. If I were to quit this minute, I am confident that I will find a way to resist any future craving to smoke, even if it gets very strong.

yes   no   not sure

If you can answer yes to all of the questions in Quiz 3, you may be a candidate for quitting immediately, cold turkey. Before you do, however, be sure to read what I have to say in this chapter just to make sure you have all the tools you will need to be successful. Then, when you finish the chapter, set a time to quit. If not that very minute, make it tomorrow, and "just do it."

What if you are like most smokers and had some doubts?

If you are like most smokers, you felt at least a small twinge of doubt when you responded to the above questions. Like most smokers, you were not completely confident that you could resist any future craving to smoke, or that you are really capable of finding something to substitute for the gratifications that cigarettes have been giving you.

In order to build the confidence you need to be a nonsmoker, (1) you must develop an arsenal of weapons to handle the immediate urge to smoke each time it hits you and (2) you must develop other ways to deal with the underlying reasons that have kept you dependent on cigarettes. During these next seven days I will show you how to accomplish both tasks, so that when your quit day comes at the end of the week (or whenever you set it) you will be completely confident that you will succeed.

HOW TO DEAL WITH THE URGE TO SMOKE AT THE TIME IT HITS YOU

YOUR SHORT-DISTANCE ARTILLERY

There are several weapons to use immediately at those moments when you have the urge to reach for a cigarette. During these next seven days, you must learn and practice all of them. EVERY ONE OF THESE WEAPONS HAS A PROVEN RECORD—THEY WORK. Some people find that one is more useful than another, but most people use several in combination or at different times. After practicing with these weapons for the next seven days, you will be able to choose the combination that will work best for you, and forget about the others.

The immediate urge to smoke usually lasts about five minutes before it passes. *If you can just resist reaching for a cigarette for five minutes, you shoot that urge down.* Of course, when you first quit, the urge comes back! But if you keep shooting it down, the period between urges will get longer and longer, and the urge will finally weaken and disappear. Many people think the word "delay" when they make a decision to resist the urge, some watch the clock for five minutes, and during that time they use one or more of the following tactics.

1. Take a deep breath, hold it a moment, and exhale as if you had taken your first drag on a cigarette. This may sound paradoxical, but part of the satisfaction that you get from a cigarette is not due directly to its nicotine content, but to the body's reaction to a deep breath. By taking a deep breath you take in a maximum amount of oxygen, and when you exhale, you expel a maximum amount of carbon dioxide. The result is a feeling of relief and relaxation. Try it right now, without "benefit" of a cigarette, and you will see what I mean. Take a full, deep breath, hold it a moment, and exhale as you might after taking the first puff of a cigarette. Notice the natural reaction of letting go in the upper part of your body, especially your shoulders. Some people like to do this several times over the five-minute period, just as if they were smoking.
2. Take a sip of water several times during this five-minute period. It lessens the desire to smoke and gives you something to do with your hands. If you are not using nicotine replacement, it also helps flush the nicotine from your body.

3. Put something else that's noncaloric in your mouth, such as a cocktail straw, a toothpick, or, possibly best yet, a piece of stick cinnamon.
4. Distract yourself. Get busy with something that will require full attention for five minutes.
5. One of the very best things you can do during this five minutes if your work normally requires sitting down is to get up and move around the entire time. Five minutes of walking about, stair climbing, or lifting some light weights not only helps the urge to smoke to pass, it also increases your energy level. In addition, *it burns the calories that were previously burned in response to nicotine stimulation.* Increasing activity for five minutes every hour, in place of a cigarette, is an important weight-management strategy.
6. If it does not lead to a yen for sweets, chew one piece of regular gum or suck one piece of hard candy, such as a lemon drop or Life Saver.
7. Use nicotine replacement therapy. (More details and advice on nicotine replacement later.)

HOW TO HANDLE THE UNDERLYING REASONS FOR SMOKING

From the second quiz in Chapter 1 you became more aware of your underlying reason or reasons for smoking. It may be for energy, to enhance pleasure and relaxation, to help cope with anxiety, anger, or stress, or simply to have something to do with your hands or to fill time when you are bored. You may have become psychologically dependent on cigarettes, feeling that you cannot do without them, even without becoming chemically addicted, unless you are also a heavy smoker.

By completing Part 1 of the 7 + 7 Program, you are already doing several things that should prove to you that you can deal with any or all of these underlying reasons for smoking. Your healthful, high-carbohydrate diet will be increasing your general energy level, as will your activity program. In addition, your change in diet and increase in activity are stimulating your body to produce more of the same neurotransmitters and hormones that are increased with the use of nicotine, and can lead to its elimination as a necessity in your life.

Here is how to develop some specific weapons for dealing with each of the underlying reasons for smoking, together with the rationale for using them.

YOUR LONG-DISTANCE ARTILLERY

How to Be a High-Energy Person without Cigarettes. People who use cigarettes to maintain or increase their energy level have become dependent on the stimulating properties of nicotine in order to stay at, or reach, some preferred level of arousal. You become dependent on a drug's action because, whenever you use it, the body secretes certain chemicals to fight its action and return you to your natural, baseline state. Because of this regulatory reaction, you will feel sub-par and listless when you miss your nicotine kick. Without nicotine, your energy level can be depressed below normal until your body recovers, which may take several days or a couple of weeks. Obviously, during this period, it is especially important to do the things that can return you to your highest energy level, without the need for nicotine.

You are already doing two things that can help you feel more alive and energetic: You are eating a healthful diet and getting daily exercise. In addition, you must make sure you get enough sleep. With respect to your diet, breakfast may be particularly important. If you have been skipping breakfast in favor of a cigarette and a cup of coffee, as many smokers do, you are much more likely to suffer the blahs in the afternoon than a non-smoker who has eaten a healthful breakfast. Skipping lunch can also lead to an afternoon low.

Five minutes of just about any exercise, including walking about, stretching, or lifting some light weights, is the short-term tactic that can give you an energy boost equivalent to a cigarette. Eating a carbohydrate snack can also give you an energy boost, but if sweet snacks turn on a craving for sweets, you should stick with the complex carbohydrates that I recommended in the previous chapter (low-fat crackers, Ryekrisp, Wasa bread, etc.).

Finally, I want to emphasize that you cannot experience maximum energy as a sedentary person. While a five-minute burst of activity can give you the energy boost of a cigarette, to reach your maximum energy potential you must engage the complete activity program I outlined in the previous chapter.

How to Relax and Enhance the Pleasure of Relaxation without Cigarettes. Paradoxically, nicotine affects pleasure centers of the brain that can enhance relaxation just as it can act as a stimulant and momentarily increase energy. The way in which nicotine affects you depends in part on your particular brain chemistry, and in part on the circumstances and situations in which you use cigarettes. That is, if you learned to use cigarettes in association with other relaxing behavior, then cigarettes come to contribute to a relaxation response.

But no one needs to be dependent on cigarettes to relax. You can do a better job of relaxing by breathing deeply, as I suggested above as a weapon to defeat the immediate urge to smoke. But better yet, you can learn to achieve a much greater degree of relaxation than you obtain from cigarettes by using a technique called deep muscular relaxation, or by learning to meditate. You can learn these techniques in a matter of minutes if you follow my directions in Appendix B.

Compared to the momentary relaxation you obtain from a cigarette, the state of relaxation you achieve from deep muscular relaxation or meditation can last throughout the day. In fact, it's been reported that smokers who begin a practice of meditation for twenty minutes each day often find that their desire for cigarettes seems to disappear gradually. Meditation leads to greater awareness of one's body. In contrast with the good feelings they experience with meditation, each time they smoke, meditators seem to become much more sensitive to the terrible impact that their cigarette is having on their lungs, hearts, and metabolism. They begin to smoke less and less, and one day they feel ready to stop completely, and do it.

One of the best ways to minimize physical and mental tension is, once again, through daily exercise. From the physical standpoint, the muscles in your body relax much more fully after being tensed in exercise than they do without exercise. I think I can prove it to you quite quickly.

Raise your shoulders up to your ears as high as you can and hold that position for a count of five. Now release and let go. Rotate your shoulders a couple of times. Do you see how much looser they feel than before? The relaxation exercises that I will show you in Appendix B will help you deal with all kinds of momentary tension and muscular tightness. With a little practice, you will be able to turn on a relaxation response instantly.

When you combine the ability to turn on a relaxation response instantaneously with your daily activity program, you will find yourself dealing with life in a more relaxed, self-confident fashion than you ever have as a smoker, and you will thus have dealt with this particular underlying reason for smoking.

How to Deal with Tension and Negative Affect without Reaching for a Cigarette. If there are many things in your life right now that are causing a great deal of tension, anxiety, or frequent anger, it would be best, of course, if you could find a way to deal with the source of these emotions rather than light up a cigarette. Short of this, however, you can learn to use other tension-reducing strategies that are much healthier than smoking. And quite likely, if you can reduce tension in this way, you may become more effective in dealing with the stressors in your life.

You may not realize it if smoking gives you a temporary release from tension, but cigarette smoking actually contributes to the overall tension and stress you experience from other circumstances in your life. That's because your body becomes stressed in between nicotine-induced reactions. First, right after smoking, your body works hard to dispose of the nicotine contained in that cigarette. Then when you reach some critical low point, both physical and mental tension increase as your need for a new dose of nicotine increases. You are actually more tense than you would normally be at this time, just before reaching for a cigarette, than if you never smoked at all.

As I discussed earlier, much of the relaxing impact of smoking comes from the act of taking a deep breath itself. Try it once again, right now, without a cigarette. The more you do this, the more effective it will become. Experiment with different ways of breathing. Some people find it is more relaxing to take that deep breath, hold it for a few seconds, and exhale very slowly; others find that exhaling quickly while they focus on releasing tension in their neck and shoulders is better. But don't exhale too fast, or you may get light-headed!

The deep muscular relaxation procedure and the special breathing exercise that is included in that procedure (Appendix B) will provide both long-term and immediate tension reduction. Together with your physical activity program, your increased feeling of well-being and self-confidence may very well help you deal with the underlying circumstances that are causing stress and tension in your life.

Dealing with Psychological Dependency. Although all forms of dependency on cigarettes have a certain chemical basis, unless you are a heavy smoker (pack a day or more) the chemical basis is not likely to be particularly strong. Discomfort or annoyance when you can't smoke, such as during an airplane trip, or the need for a cigarette in certain social situations is mostly psychological. In the next seven days I will give you some practice that will give you the power to eliminate psychological dependence.

Dealing with Chemical Dependency on Nicotine. I strongly recommend that you consult your physician about nicotine replacement therapy if you smoke a pack a day or more. While research shows that, taken by itself, nicotine replacement may not lead to significantly better success rates in remaining a non-smoker a year or two down the line, it may prove to be the critical factor in getting you through the first few days after you quit smoking. Nicotine replacement significantly reduces the extent and intensity of withdrawal reactions. In addition, it can compensate at least in part, perhaps as much as 50 percent, for the reduction in metabolic rate and those other physiological changes that can lead to weight gain when you quit. This will give you the chance to use all the other short- and long-term weapons in the 7 + 7 Program to fight the underlying reasons for your addiction and make sure you will be able to live happily and permanently without cigarettes in the future. See the special section in which I discuss the use of nicotine gum on page 93.

Keeping Hands Busy and Fighting Boredom. While it may not be the primary reason for smoking, doing something with your hands, like lighting and handling a cigarette, can become part of a person's habitual reactions in certain situations. Some people automatically reach for a cigarette when they arrive at a party, enter a bar, make a phone call, or are forced to wait for something or someone without anything else handy to engage their attention. Some people fill time with smoking when they can't think of anything else to do.

If this description applies to you, you must find different ways to replace the mechanical act of smoking. Some people find it helpful to adopt a particular behavior that can have symbolic value; each time they do it in place of smoking they can feel positive about themselves because it means they are being successful in resisting a cigarette. Sipping water, using a toothpick or cocktail straw in place of a cigarette, working on the daily crossword puzzle in the newspaper, knitting, or fingering a special coin or medallion can come to represent and symbolize your determination not to smoke.

If boredom is sometimes an issue for you, consider whether quitting smoking can be a time in which you pick up on a hobby or avocation that you have always wanted to pursue, or which you have been neglecting. It would be great if smoking didn't go well with such an activity! Perhaps working on a puzzle, knitting, or playing a computer game could become an interesting, relaxing way to fill otherwise empty time.

THE SEVEN-DAY PROGRAM TO QUIT SMOKING

NICOTINE INTERACTS WITH MANY OTHER DRUGS. IF YOU ARE TAKING ANY PRESCRIPTION OR OVER-THE-COUNTER MEDICATION, BE SURE TO INFORM YOUR PHYSICIAN THAT YOU ARE ABOUT TO QUIT SMOKING.

The first thing you must do to set the actual process of quitting in motion is to set an official quit date. While you can be flexible, depending on how you feel during these next seven days, I recommend one week from today. Seven days will give you all the time you need to practice with your anti-smoking weaponry and to demonstrate to yourself that you can be a successful quitter. On the eighth day, it's all systems go.

DAYS 1 AND 2

Monitor your smoking behavior for two days. Each time you smoke, ask yourself this short set of questions:

1. Why am I smoking this cigarette?
2. If I chose to, would this be an easy one or a difficult one to do without?
3. If I decided not to smoke this particular cigarette, what would I do instead?

Although many people who quit on their own just make mental notes of the time, place, and reasons for smoking, and begin to plan how they will deal with each situation, you are likely to be more successful if you keep a written record. Use the Smoking Record at the end of this chapter.

It's best to keep your record as you smoke each cigarette, since it will force you to review all the suggestions I have made, and plan carefully. However, if this is inconvenient, take time at the end of the day and review your smoking behavior again. Recall as many of the situations in which you smoked, and think seriously about your plans for dealing with each.[1]

If you have been smoking as a way to cope with stress or negative emotions, be sure to practice the relaxation or meditation technique in Appendix B each day.

---

[1]Some people find it helpful to wrap a piece of notepaper around their pack of cigarettes and fasten it with Scotch tape. They keep their smoking record on this piece of paper.

Day 3

It's time to test and hone your weapons. Use your short-range artillery to shoot down the urge to smoke *at least once today*. Start with a cigarette that you rated "easy" during the two-day monitoring period, and do it at a time when you can test out as many of your weapons as possible. During the five-minute period that it will take for the urge to smoke to pass, try out one or more of the following weapons until you find your own best combination:

1. Take a deep breath as though smoking, and repeat as necessary.
2. Sip water.
3. Suck on a straw, toothpick, or cinnamon stick.
4. Eat ONE piece of hard candy or chew ONE piece of gum.
5. Distract yourself—get busy with something that requires five minutes of your undivided attention.
6. Get up and walk about or lift light weights.
7. Try out a piece of nicotine gum, if you have decided to use nicotine replacement therapy.

Begin to develop this attitude: "If I can skip one cigarette, I can skip them all." And you *will* be able to skip them all as you continue to hone the use of your weapons these next several days.

You can, of course, decide to skip more than one cigarette today, and it will get easier and easier if you think of it only as a game, something like one of those arcade or computer games in which you shoot down evil monsters. Only, in this case, the evil monsters are cigarettes.

As in those arcade or computer games, it can take a while until you master the strategy and tactics to win. So if you fail in any given effort to skip a cigarette, just go back to your war room and replot your strategy.

If all of this comes easy to you, just keep track of your progress mentally. Every success is a victory over a powerful drug. However, I think you will find it helpful to continue to keep a record of your smoking behavior today and for the rest of the week as you did the first two days. The record will help you plan your future course of action in each of the situations in which you smoke.

Be sure to continue to practice relaxation or meditation each day if you are using one of these strategies to deal with your underlying reasons for smoking.

Day 4

Today is another test day. If you haven't already jumped the gun and tried it on Day 3, it's time to skip *at least one cigarette* that you rated "difficult" during your two-day monitoring period.

Keep your Smoking Record and if you fail in your effort to skip a difficult cigarette you must avoid kicking yourself. This is a practice period and you are experimenting with your various weapons in order to learn how to be effective.

In case you found skipping that cigarette very difficult, or did, indeed, fail in the end, review carefully everything that got in the way of your being successful. The most common things that quitters face which lead to difficulty or failure, together with some possible remedies, include:

The chemical aspects of addiction: When you skip cigarettes you feel lousy! *Remedy:* If you are a heavy smoker, once again I encourage you to use nicotine replacement therapy if you have not already decided to do so.

Social pressure: You found yourself in a situation in which you and your friends are engaging in an activity (cocktail party, coffee break) in which you normally smoke. *Remedy:* Tell everyone who might have a negative impact on your desire to quit smoking of your serious intentions *and why it is important to you.* If they are really your friends, and even if they are smokers themselves, they will avoid doing anything that might encourage you to join them. You may also find it helpful to enlist a special non-smoking buddy for social support, someone with whom you can talk things over during this quitting period. Just be sure you tell this person what might be helpful to you and what might not, since even with the best intentions your friend may say or do things that just make the situation worse. Finally, in this regard, you must ask yourself, "If I continue to face this kind of social situation, will I really be able to quit? Do I need to avoid such situations for a certain period of time, until I become fully confident that I can be a non-smoker forever?" If you feel that you will not be able to resist the social pressure to smoke, and you are serious about quitting, you must avoid such situations for about two or three weeks, until the urge to smoke is gone.

Extreme tension or negative emotion: Something beyond the usual ordinary stress of daily living, a crisis, occurs in your work or personal life, and one of your underlying reasons for smoking has been for tension reduction or relaxation. *Remedy:* This may require a combination of remedies.

First, as a basis for dealing with negative emotions, redouble your efforts to use the tension-reduction weapons I have already given you. Get away from the particular environment with which the tension is directly associated—go to another room or take a walk. Use your relaxation strategy. Second, you may find that nicotine replacement therapy in the form of the gum, which has some of the same cyclic effect of cigarettes, provides enough tension relief to get you through your immediate reaction. Third, talk out your problems with a sympathetic listener. It's better to blow off steam than to inhale cigarette smoke. Start with a person or relation with whom you are friendly. If that doesn't help, think about talking it over with your minister, priest, or rabbi. Finally, if you really cannot find a way to deal with the stressors in your life, except as a smoker, these stressors are probably serious enough for you to consult a health professional, or you may never be able to have a happy, healthier life.

DAYS 5, 6, AND 7
This is the home stretch.

Your main objective in these next three days is to end up on Day 7 smoking about half the number of cigarettes you used to smoke before you began Part 2 of the 7 + 7 Program. If you used to smoke a full pack, you aim for about ten cigarettes on Day 7.[2] Fewer is even better.

[2] If you normally smoke a high- or medium-nicotine brand of cigarettes, some experts suggest that you switch to a brand one step lower in nicotine content as a way to cut your nicotine intake prior to complete smoking cessation. Or you may try switching from regular to menthol, or vice versa, to make cigarettes less attrac-

In order to reach your objective for Day 7, set a target for Days 5 and 6, cutting out a few cigarettes each day in a way that will move you gradually toward your goal. This attenuation permits a gradual withdrawal from nicotine and should make quitting easier. Maintain your Smoking Record during these three days and keep practicing with those tactics that seem most helpful to you.

At some point during these three days you may feel like jumping the gun and quitting before your official quit date. You're the boss and the moment you feel confident that you can succeed, "just do it."

But what if you still have doubts?

If this occurs, the underlying reason in all likelihood is your dependence on the chemical impact of nicotine. It's a very powerful drug, and many forces have been operating to make you addicted. Since you have come this far, I urge you once again to discuss immediately with your physician the use of nicotine replacement therapy. It can significantly reduce withdrawal symptoms and can get you over the hump. Remember, nicotine itself is not carcinogenic. It's the hook that has gotten you to smoke cigarettes, which carry numerous other substances that are dangerous to your health. With the help of either the patch or nicotine gum, you will have all the other weapons you need from the 7 + 7 Program to be a successful quitter.

Your physician will give you advice on how to use the

---

tive in flavor. The problem with this approach is that it maintains the habit aspects of smoking in the many situations in which you may smoke, and, in addition, can lead to inhaling more deeply or more often with each cigarette in order to maximize your nicotine intake.

patch. Normally, a heavy smoker might use the patch for up to six weeks, starting first with a patch that contains a high dose of nicotine. The nicotine is released slowly throughout the day and the nicotine content of your bloodstream tends to be about 50 percent of what it might be if you continued to smoke. Every two weeks, the dose is reduced. Typically, heavy smokers start with a 21-milligram patch, reduce it to 14 milligrams after two weeks, and then finish up with a 7-milligram patch. DO NOT SMOKE while you are using the patch or you may experience a dangerous overdose of nicotine.

The patch may be most useful for smokers who start early in the day and continue on a fairly regular basis, since it releases nicotine on a continual, gradual basis. If you tend to concentrate your smoking at one particular time every day, say at night, and only smoke lightly if at all during the rest of the day, a continuous release of nicotine may cause discomfort (dizziness or headaches) during the time when you are not accustomed to smoking very much. The gum would be more suitable in these circumstances. Also, a small percentage of users suffer from local irritation or itchiness from the patch.

HOW TO USE NICOTINE GUM

When you use nicotine gum, chewing a piece every hour or whenever you have the urge to smoke, you tend to mimic the cyclic rise and fall of nicotine in your system that occurs when you smoke cigarettes. I was impressed by the impact of the gum when I tried it. I felt the same kind of "hit" that I used to get from cigarettes. Of course, I'm no longer a smoker, so the magnitude of the effect was more like the one you get from a cigarette after not smoking for a day or two.

The gum is available in 2- or 4-milligram doses and, at the time of this writing, only with a doctor's prescription (it may soon become available without). Normally, the higher dose is recommended only for heavy smokers when they first quit smoking, and is then reduced.

You can use up to thirty pieces of the 2-milligram gum a day, although most people average between twelve and sixteen. The upper limit for the 4-milligram gum is twenty pieces, and the average is ten. Because of the danger of remaining addicted to nicotine and the greater likelihood of side effects (discussed below), many experts shy away from recommending the 4-milligram gum, and I, too, suggest you use the 2-milligram gum, unless your physician recommends otherwise.

If you use the gum, use it to the extent it can be helpful in combination with certain of your other anti-smoking weapons. Take a deep breath, or walk around for five minutes (but do not drink liquid while the gum is in your mouth because it will reduce its effectiveness and possibly upset your stomach). You can use the 2-milligram gum each time you feel the urge to smoke, or on a schedule such as every hour if you are not a particularly heavy smoker (it will help minimize withdrawal symptoms).

Although some experts suggest you wait until quit day to begin using the gum, I think you will do better if you begin to experiment and get used to using it during Part 2 of the

7 + 7 Program. Substitute a piece of gum for one or two (*but not more*) of the cigarettes that you are beginning to omit each day. The reasons for substituting gum for only one or two cigarettes during this period, and not for all of them, are to make sure you don't overdose yourself on nicotine and to make sure that the amount of nicotine that's present in your system when you quit has been lowered.

Here are specific instructions for maximizing the effectiveness of nicotine gum (in the 2-milligram dose).

WHEN TO USE

Chew a piece each time you feel the urge to smoke.

Wait at least fifteen minutes after drinking coffee, tea, milk, fruit juices, or cola beverages before using the gum. The acid in the drinks reduces the effectiveness of the gum.

If the taste of the gum is not offensive first thing in the morning, you can start chewing right after waking, including first thing in the morning on quit day.

HOW TO USE

Chew the gum very slowly until you taste it. Chew just once or twice and wait a moment to see if the taste becomes evident. If not, chew again.

When the taste appears, place the nicotine gum between your cheek and your gum line.

After the flavor disappears, take a chew or two until you taste it again, and put the gum back in your cheek. This should occur every minute or two.

Chew each piece of gum for not less than twenty and up to thirty minutes, then throw it away.

Do not drink any liquids while the gum is in your mouth.

How Much to Use

Use ten to thirty pieces of gum each day.

Do not use more than thirty pieces a day.

As the urge to smoke eases, gradually reduce the number of pieces used each day.

However, do not underuse the gum during the first week of quitting if you sense any significant withdrawal symptoms, especially cigarette cravings. Correct use significantly reduces withdrawal symptoms.

Most people can be finished with the gum in one month or less, but you can continue to use it for up to six months.

Side Effects

Some people experience a sore jaw, irritation of the mouth, heartburn, nausea, or hiccups. These usually can be prevented by chewing the gum more slowly. Some people object to the taste of the gum itself when they chew for a full half hour. If this occurs in your case, try chewing for only twenty-five minutes (not less than twenty minutes for a reasonably full impact) and on a schedule of once an hour. Resist any urge to smoke between pieces of gum with one of your other smoke-resisting weapons.

WARNING: Pregnant or lactating women should not

use the gum. Smokers with any form of heart disease should use the gum only on the advice and under the close supervision of their physician.

SPECIAL ADVICE FOR QUIT DAY

Unless you are completely confident that the presence and sight of a cigarette will not provide a stimulus to smoke, I think you should get rid of all smoking paraphernalia, at least temporarily. Throw away or give away all cigarettes, ashtrays, cigarette lighters, and matches in your home and workplace. There is no need to force yourself to resist temptation when it is staring you right in the face. Almost every ex-smoker that I spoke with told me that they failed to quit when they kept cigarettes in their home or office. They usually persuaded themselves that "just this one" would not hurt. But it did. Once you are a confident non-smoker you may be able to have cigarettes around without danger of relapsing, but then, why would you want to?

In spite of all your excellent preparation you may still experience some withdrawal symptoms. Be prepared. They may last only a day or two, or as long as two to four weeks.

The 7 + 7 Program will have prepared you to deal with changes in appetite and the craving for cigarettes that smokers face when they quit. Here are some ways to cope with the other typical withdrawal symptoms.

> *Dizziness* may occur during the first day or two. It may last a few moments at a time. Take a rest—it will pass.

Headaches may occur anytime during the first few weeks. Relax, take your usual headache medication, try a cold compress on the back of your neck. Slight tension headaches can sometimes be relieved by taking a walk.

Tiredness can occur during the first two to four weeks, but is not likely if you maintain your exercise program, take time for a relaxation or meditation period once or twice a day, and get enough sleep.

Coughing may actually increase for a day or two after quitting, as your lungs get rid of the smoking residue that coats them. The cough will disappear gradually over several days. It helps to sip water or suck a cough drop or piece of hard candy.

Tightness in the chest may occur during the first week. Take a rest and breathe deeply—it will pass.

Trouble sleeping may occur the first few days. Do not drink caffeinated beverages late in the day, do not do strenuous or prolonged physical activity during the two hours before going to sleep, drink a glass of milk or eat a bowl of cereal with milk as your nighttime snack, and take a hot bath before retiring.

Constipation may occur during the first two to four weeks after quitting, but is not likely if you are following the nutrition advice in Part 1 of the 7 + 7 Program. Eating a high-fiber diet (fruits, vegetables, and grain foods), drinking plenty of water, and getting at least forty-five minutes of physical activity are your best safeguards.

Difficulty concentrating may occur during the first few weeks. Be prepared for this; take a break and do something physical for a few minutes.

OTHER PHARMACOLOGICAL AIDS TO SMOKING CESSATION AND WEIGHT MANAGEMENT

Depending upon your needs, there are a number of other pharmacological aids that your physician may recommend to help minimize withdrawal symptoms and manage your weight. Some are available without a prescription, but should not be used when you quit smoking without consulting your doctor. These include:

1. Fenfluramine. This prescription drug stimulates serotonin secretion to control appetite and sweet cravings, and has a tendency to increase your metabolic rate.
2. Phenylpropanolamine. This drug, found in prescription and over-the-counter weight-management and cold symptom medications, may have an appetite-suppressing effect.
3. Other appetite suppressants that might be prescribed by your physician for a brief period include benzphetamine, diethylpropion, mazindol, phendimetrazine, phenmetrazine, and phentermine. These drugs lose their effectiveness in a short time and occasionally cause serious side effects. They should be monitored by your physician.
4. The amino acid tryptophan may also have an appetite-suppressing effect since it increases the activity of serotonin. One study reported an effective dosage of 50 milligrams per kilogram of body weight daily.
5. Some persons, typically heavy smokers, feel depressed when they quit smoking. Prozac, while not appearing to have any effect on a person's weight, has been found useful in preventing serious depression.

A WORD ABOUT CAFFEINE AND ALCOHOL

Since nicotine is a central nervous system stimulant, you may be wondering if you could substitute caffeine for nicotine. *Don't do it.*

If you customarily drink several cups of coffee, tea, or other beverages containing caffeine, BE VERY CAREFUL NOT TO INCREASE YOUR CONSUMPTION! Nicotine suppresses the effect of caffeine, cutting some of its stimulating properties in half or even a little more. Thus, when you quit smoking, the impact of caffeine increases. If you drink more than a couple of cups of coffee, tea, or other caffeinated beverages every day, and continue to do so after you quit smoking, you may actually find yourself getting jittery so that you'll have to cut back. (Unfortunately, in spite of an increase in the impact of caffeine on your nerves when you quit smoking, it does not seem to compensate for the metabolic changes that occur which cause weight gain.)

If, however, as a smoker you have not been drinking beverages containing caffeine, you might consult with your doctor about using prescription or over-the-counter caffeine tablets. As a person who has not previously used caffeine, there is some possibility that it can have a stimulating effect on your metabolic rate. But I would not advise a person to develop a caffeine habit to replace the nicotine habit. Caffeine can also cause some undesirable side effects, such as nervousness, diarrhea, dizziness, fast heartbeat, and trouble sleeping. And if you start to drink coffee as a way to obtain caffeine, you may end up with a sour stomach and heartburn.

Alcohol, in contrast with nicotine and caffeine, has a sedating effect. If you smoke when you drink, the stimulating properties of nicotine can counter, to a certain extent, the sedating effects of alcohol. When you quit smoking the sedating or intoxicating impact of alcohol will therefore increase. If you consume more than a modest amount of alcohol, you should cut back. *Alcohol should always be used in moderation by people concerned with their weight.* While the mechanism is not completely understood, alcohol facilitates fat storage. As a former smoker and person interested in managing your weight, you should restrict your intake to one or two glasses of wine, or the equivalent, per day.

And now, CONGRATULATIONS!

You have finished the 7 + 7 Program of *How to Quit Smoking without Gaining Weight.* I want to wish you good luck in your efforts to remain a non-smoker and good health in the years to come.

If, in the future, you experience any difficulty managing your weight using the general nutrition advice I have given you in Part 1 of the 7 + 7 Program and the diet you have designed for yourself based on this advice, go directly to the next chapter and follow the explicit daily menu plan in the Ex-Smoker's Weight-Management Program.

SOME WORDS OF ADVICE AND ENCOURAGEMENT FROM EX-SMOKERS

During the months in which I was writing this book I interviewed a number of ex-smokers, asking them what the key factors were in motivating them to quit smoking, and what strategies they used to be successful in preventing weight gain as well as in quitting.

Karen Ashworth, an executive with a public relations firm, expressed well the common fears and wishes that we all experienced as smokers and which motivated us to quit. "I watched my father go in and out of the hospital. He has emphysema and suffers repeatedly from pneumonia. He can hardly breathe sometimes, and walking even a short distance is nearly impossible. He has to give himself breathing treatments every four hours with his portable breathing machine. He keeps saying to me, 'If I only knew what I know now thirty years ago.' Well, I know it and I quit last year on July 5th, at the very age my father would have been if he had quit thirty years ago."

When I asked Karen what she did to maintain her weight, besides mentioning the low-fat substitutions she was making, Karen said, "Drinking water was most important when I quit. I carried a half-gallon jug to work, and sipped every time I thought about smoking when I first quit, but then I discovered it was the best thing to do to keep from eating unnecessarily, too. I still carry a jug every day." As for exercise, in addition to using every opportunity to move around during the working day, Karen told me, "I do about thirty minutes a day. I alternate between step aerobics [she has a videotape], an exercise bicycle, and a stair climber. But I'm always fighting five extra pounds." I think it's going to take a little more physical activity to take care of anyone's last five pounds, but I think you can consider yourself successful if you, too, can do as well as Karen.

In my own case, I quit smoking cigarettes habitually in 1953 when the research I had been studying convinced me that cigarettes caused cancer. But I switched to cigars and continued to smoke them, one or two a day, as well as a cigarette perhaps once a month, until one day in the spring of 1983. As I was cleaning the cigar-smoke film that coated the inside windshield of my car, I suddenly became very conscious that that same film was coating my lungs even though I was not inhaling cigar smoke directly. It was on my mind when I was talking with my wife in our den and reached for a cigar later that same day. At that moment the thought occurred to me that I was killing her with cigar smoke, as well as myself. I did not light that cigar, and have never lit one since. After about two days, I did not miss smoking at all, and it was certainly motivating to see the cough that I had developed begin to disappear. Since I was already a very active person, playing competitive tennis several times a week and jogging about 25 miles a week, I did not regain any of the 70 pounds I had previously lost in 1963.

My literary agent, Richard Pine, quit smoking seventeen years ago, at the age of twenty-two. When I asked him what motivated him he told me, "I tried to quit a few times in college, but failed. I had a smoker's cough, which reminded me all was not completely well inside my chest, but I began to smoke more right after college. A little more than a pack a day became two-plus and I began experiencing side effects I didn't like: losing a step or two on the basketball court and a thickening of my saliva. They bothered me an awful lot. I thought of quitting every morning and began to have nightmares of falling asleep with a cigarette in my hand. Over the course of a few months I became absolutely certain that I was well on the road to emphysema or cancer. I had visions of myself lying in the hospital, unconscious and connected to a jungle of tubes and machines that barely kept me alive. So, I came to the point where I knew I had to make a choice: keep smoking and die a painful, ugly death sometime in the near future, or quit and live a long life." Richard was always thin and never did overeat, and being very active—walking a lot, riding a bicycle, and playing basketball—he never gained weight when he quit. And he is just as slim today as the day I met him in the summer of 1981.

In spite of being a smoker, Ben Wilson, who is a minister at one of our local churches, had never been able to manage his weight. He was fifty-two years old and weighed 255 pounds when the need to make what had become an annual trip to the tailor to alter his clothes finally convinced him it was time to change. It was on his way home from the tailor that day, in December 1991, with his newly enlarged wardrobe, that he decided to follow *The T-Factor Diet,* which he had heard about, but never used. I talked with him about his weight and smoking experiences on February 2, 1994, a few days after one of his parishioners told me about his success story.

"The first thing I did when I got home that day [in 1991] was throw out the candy and the colas that I knew were contributing to my problem. I didn't want them around the house to tempt me. I had also been cooking up a batch of fried fish or chicken about three times a week. Now I bake or broil, but I don't deny myself completely. Occasionally I do indulge in a hamburger, but it's not very often."

Because his ever-increasing weight was contributing to the deterioration of his knee joints, and he was ultimately going to need surgery, Ben's doctor advised him that he should not attempt a vigorous aerobic program that might cause further damage, but that he should focus on strength training for his upper body and include the leg exercises that would be important for rehabilitation after surgery. However, short periods of walking at a moderate pace were just fine, so, to burn calories, his doctor advised him to simply walk whenever he could throughout the day. Ben said, "I rarely sit still for any length of time—I use every excuse to walk."

Ben decided to quit smoking about one year later, after he had lost over 50 pounds. "I weighed about 205 pounds when I quit smoking and I decided to use the nicotine patch to help me with the urge to smoke and maybe my weight. But I already knew what I needed to do [for my weight]—stick to a low-fat diet and keep exercising, so I quit using the patches after fourteen days." Fortunately, Ben's strength-training program, which he does for thirty-five minutes three times a week at a fitness center, his wake-up routine which includes 100 stomach crunches every morning, and his walking about whenever he finds a chance throughout the day seem to be just the right balance of physical activity, since this combination of exercises increases the burning of both fat and glucose in his fuel mixture.

"I continued to lose weight after I quit smoking by following *The T-Factor Diet* and keeping up with my exercise. With *The T-Factor Diet* I already had my appetite under control and it never became a problem. But someone told me to drink a lot of water after I quit smoking and I think that helped flush the nicotine out of my system and reduced my desire to smoke. I lost another 25 pounds after I quit smoking and my weight stays now between 178 and 180 pounds."

Ben told me that he has no trouble maintaining his weight, so I congratulated Ben again and wished him continued success. He quickly responded to my good wishes with, "You don't need to worry. I work at this. I *mean* to do it, I mean to succeed." I wish you could have heard the calm determination in his voice as he made these last remarks.

Harry Gillis is sixty-eight years old and recently retired from his position as a vice-president at a bank in Nashville. "I'd been a pack-a-day smoker for forty years, and had made many efforts to stop, but it never lasted too long. Finally, I enrolled in a smoking-cessation clinic at a local hospital in July 1990. This time I made up my mind to quit. I think that's necessary—you really have to make up your mind to quit."

I asked Harry to give me some details about the program and he said, "As part of the program we had to record the time, place, and reason why we were smoking each cigarette. It was such a terrible bother that I just quit, cold turkey, without waiting for the group's quit date. I've never smoked since. The thing that helped me most was the group support. I was getting a divorce at the time, and without the group's influence I think the stress would have driven me back to cigarettes. When I went to a follow-up meeting in February 1991, several of the others had started smoking again. They thought they could have just one now and then, and pretty soon they were back on cigarettes. I don't think you can do that. At least I don't think I could, so I never have. I don't keep any stuff around the house, either, but I have one friend who has kept his last pack of cigarettes in his freezer for ten years, and never smoked. Pretty amazing, I think."

When I asked Harry about his weight, he told me, "Exercise made the big difference for me. During the program I exercised for two hours a day and lost 25 pounds. Five times a week I would go to the fitness center at the hospital and I walked on those days, too. Now I just walk for 4 miles every morning."

I could go on with many such stories, each a bit different, but all will share one central, common feature—the need for exercise if you want to manage your weight. The last story puts it very well, and was told to me by Bob Billings, a Nashville attorney. "I had tried for many years to quit smoking before I was finally successful in February 1992. And, in spite of being a smoker, my weight had also fluctuated, up and down, as much as 25 pounds. This time, when I quit, I had my exercise program firmly in place.[3] I had joined the exercise program at the Dayani Center[4] in the fall of 1991, and I was going three or four times a week. To make sure I was active every day, I bought a Nordic Track for the home. When I decided to quit smoking I had already lost 7 pounds and I was feeling pretty good about myself because I was exercising. I used the patch when I quit smoking and the patch made me feel even better. I used it for six weeks,

[3]Bob was the first person to use the expression "firmly in place" with respect to his exercise program. I liked it so well that I used it myself elsewhere in this book.
[4]The Dayani Human Performance Center at Vanderbilt University offers smoking-cessation programs through its Institute for Smoking Prevention and Cessation.

YOUR GUARANTEE

If you have faithfully followed the program in *How to Quit Smoking without Gaining Weight* and find after you have stopped smoking cigarettes that you have gained more than the amount of weight that can be accounted for in the normal daily fluctuations due to variation in water retention (3 to 5 pounds), and you wish the money you paid for this book returned under this money-back guarantee, please send the sales receipt and either the original or a photocopy of the eating and activity records for the first three weeks after you quit smoking and the last three weeks prior to your claim, together with a record of your weight at the beginning and end of each three-week period, to Department PJC at W. W. Norton & Company, Inc., 500 Fifth Avenue, New York, NY 10110. Please be sure that these records are complete and that they show that you have given the program a fair trial. This guarantee is good for ninety days after the date on the sales receipt. For our research purposes, please indicate whether you used nicotine gum or the patch as an aid to quitting smoking. (Your answer to this question does not affect your guarantee.) Also, please list any medications that you are taking on a regular basis. Since many medications have weight gain as an undesirable side effect, this warranty is void if you do not consult your physician and make any adjustment in your medication that is deemed necessary as a consequence of your withdrawal from nicotine.

starting with a 21-milligram patch for two weeks, 14 milligrams for the next two weeks, and ending with 7 milligrams. I'm now another 12 pounds lighter and I have been off cigarettes for a year."

Now it's your turn.

I like to receive letters with success stories and I have received literally thousands as a result of my weight-management books. But I also will respond with advice when people are having trouble following my recommendations. Please do not call on the telephone, but you can write, if you wish, to:

> Martin Katahn, Ph.D.
> 4607 Belmont Park Terrace
> Nashville, TN 37215

Whether it's for advice, encouragement, or just to tell me your success story, I look forward to hearing from you.

SMOKING RECORD

Instructions. Use the top section of each page to record cigarettes actually smoked during each of the next seven days. Record the time, place and with whom, reason, whether it will be an easy (E) or difficult (D) cigarette to eliminate, and the anti-smoking weapon or weapons you plan to use to eliminate that cigarette. *Use the bottom section* of each page as you begin to eliminate cigarettes, beginning on Day 3. Record the time and other information each time you make a decision to eliminate a particular cigarette. Indicate what anti-smoking weapon you practiced with. In the comments section indicate whether or not you were successful, and the reason why in either case. In case of failure, plan what you will do next time.

Day 1 · CIGARETTES SMOKED

DATE:

No.	TIME	PLACE & WITH WHOM	REASON FOR SMOKING	E OR D	WEAPON TO USE
1					
2					
3					
4					
5					
6					
7					
8					
9					
10					
11					
12					
13					
14					
15					
16					
17					
18					
19					
20					

No.	Time	Place & with Whom	Reason for Smoking	E or D	Weapon to Use
21					
22					
23					
24					
25					
26					
27					
28					
29					
30					
31					
32					
33					
34					
35					
36					
37					
38					
39					
40					

Day 2 · CIGARETTES SMOKED

DATE:

No.	Time	Place & with Whom	Reason for Smoking	E or D	Weapon to Use
1					
2					
3					
4					
5					
6					
7					
8					
9					
10					
11					
12					
13					
14					
15					
16					
17					
18					
19					
20					

No.	Time	Place & With Whom	Reason for Smoking	E or D	Weapon to Use
21					
22					
23					
24					
25					
26					
27					
28					
29					
30					
31					
32					
33					
34					
35					
36					
37					
38					
39					
40					

Day 3 · CIGARETTES SMOKED

DATE:

No.	TIME	PLACE & WITH WHOM	REASON FOR SMOKING	E OR D	WEAPON TO USE
1					
2					
3					
4					
5					
6					
7					
8					
9					
10					
11					
12					
13					
14					
15					
16					
17					
18					
19					
20					
21					
22					

No.	Time	Place & with Whom	Reason for Smoking	E or D	Weapon to Use
23					
24					
25					
26					
27					
28					
29					
30					
31					
32					
33					
34					
35					
36					
37					
38					

CIGARETTES ELIMINATED

No.	Time	Place & with Whom	Weapon(s) Used	E or D	Comments
1					
2					
3					
4					
5					

Day 4 · CIGARETTES SMOKED

DATE:

No.	Time	Place & with Whom	Reason for Smoking	E or D	Weapon to Use
1					
2					
3					
4					
5					
6					
7					
8					
9					
10					
11					
12					
13					
14					
15					
16					
17					
18					
19					
20					
21					
22					
23					

No.	Time	Place & with Whom	Reason for Smoking	E or D	Weapon to Use
24					
25					
26					
27					
28					
29					
30					
31					
32					
33					
34					
35					

CIGARETTES ELIMINATED

No.	Time	Place & with Whom	Weapon(s) Used	E or D	Comments
1					
2					
3					
4					
5					
6					
7					
8					
9					
10					

D a y   5 · CIGARETTES SMOKED

DATE:

No.	TIME	PLACE & WITH WHOM	REASON FOR SMOKING	E OR D	WEAPON TO USE
1					
2					
3					
4					
5					
6					
7					
8					
9					
10					
11					
12					
13					
14					
15					
16					
17					
18					
19					
20					

No.	Time	Place & with Whom	Reason for Smoking	E or D	Weapon to Use	
21						
22						
23						
24						
25						
26						
27						
28						
29						
30						

CIGARETTES ELIMINATED

No.	Time	Place & with Whom	Weapon(s) Used	E or D	Comments	
1						
2						
3						
4						
5						
6						
7						
8						
9						
10						

Day 6 · CIGARETTES SMOKED

DATE:

No.	Time	Place & with Whom	Reason for Smoking	E or D	Weapon to Use
1					
2					
3					
4					
5					
6					
7					
8					
9					
10					
11					
12					
13					
14					
15					
16					
17					
18					
19					
20					

No.	Time	Place & with Whom	Reason for Smoking	E or D	Weapon to Use
21					
22					
23					
24					
25					

CIGARETTES ELIMINATED

No.	Time	Place & with Whom	Weapon(s) Used	E or D	Comments
1					
2					
3					
4					
5					
6					
7					
8					
9					
10					
11					
12					
13					
14					
15					

Day 7 · CIGARETTES SMOKED

DATE:

No.	TIME	PLACE & WITH WHOM	REASON FOR SMOKING	E OR D	WEAPON TO USE
1					
2					
3					
4					
5					
6					
7					
8					
9					
10					
11					
12					
13					
14					
15					
16					
17					
18					
19					
20					

CIGARETTES ELIMINATED

No.	Time	Place & with Whom	Weapon(s) Used	E or D	Comments
1					
2					
3					
4					
5					
6					
7					
8					
9					
10					
11					
12					
13					
14					
15					
16					
17					
18					
19					
20					

5

THE EX-SMOKER'S WEIGHT-MANAGEMENT PROGRAM

If you are a former smoker who's gained weight after quitting, don't despair. You'll be able to lose it quite painlessly by following the advice in this chapter.

Former smokers who have been off cigarettes long enough to feel confident that they are in no danger of relapsing can begin immediately with the Ex-Smoker's Weight-Management Program on page 126.

But what if you have just recently quit, still crave cigarettes, and, to top it off, find that you are gaining weight?

If you have just recently quit and are still fighting the urge to resume smoking, it's best to move gradually into a weight-management program. Trying to change your dietary habits too quickly can add to the stress you may still be experiencing in your efforts to remain a non-smoker and only increase your craving for cigarettes. Your highest priority at this time should be *to remain a non-smoker*.

Aim first to stop gaining weight, and once you've accomplished that, think about what additional steps it will take to lose weight. The best way to do this without impairing your ability to remain a non-smoker is to use the following strategy.

1. Increase your physical activity. This is more important in the total picture right now than changing your diet because the more active you become, the easier it will be to remain a non-smoker as well as to manage your weight. Review my advice on pages 65–71 and set a target of at least forty-five minutes a day.

2. Then begin to cut the fat in your diet. Start by making low-fat substitutions for the high-fat foods in accordance with my meal and snack suggestions in Chapter 3. Keep track of your daily fat-gram intake. Move gradually toward the daily fat-gram target in the Ex-Smoker's Weight-Management Program described below. If you are able, in time, to reach the target level for weight loss comfortably, without endangering your ability to remain a non-smoker, you should begin to lose weight.

3. If increasing your activity and cutting the fat as I recommend do not prevent further weight gain and start you on the road to losing weight, as it will in almost all cases, you may be consuming too much carbohydrate. Monitor your carbohydrate intake to determine if you are overdoing sweets independently of fat, that is, eating more than one piece of hard candy or any other sugar candy in place of a cigarette, or more than one serving of a complex carbohydrate at snack times. Study my advice on carbohydrate foods in Chapter 3. You'll find some other suggestions below.

4. Discuss with your doctor the use of nicotine replacement,

with the patch or gum, or the use of one of the pharmacological aids to smoking cessation and weight control I discussed on page 99. These aids serve a dual purpose since, like increasing physical activity, they work simultaneously to ensure your success in remaining a non-smoker and in managing your weight.

5. Continue to use whatever smoking-cessation strategies are helping you to deal with your desire to smoke until you are safely through the transition to becoming a fully successful non-smoker. Then begin the Ex-Smoker's Weight-Management Program, which contains detailed daily menus and a daily fat-gram target that will help you gradually and permanently lose whatever weight you have gained.

THE EX-SMOKER'S WEIGHT-MANAGEMENT PROGRAM

The amount of fat on your body is adjusted primarily by the amount of fat in your diet.

If you increase or decrease the amount of fat in your diet, you gain or lose a certain percentage of fat from your body. Each of us has a certain range over which this occurs rather easily. It's genetically determined. For the rare person with real skinny genes, perhaps one in twenty, the range may be only a few pounds either way no matter how much fat that person eats. But for most of us, the range is more like 20 to 50 pounds. And for those of us with a strong genetic tendency toward obesity, it can be 100 pounds or even several hundred pounds in extreme cases.

Of course, physical activity narrows the range. An ultra-marathon runner, who runs 50- or 100-mile races several times a year, and who runs over 10 miles a day in training, will tend to burn off whatever fat he eats before it can settle in his fat cells. But at lesser daily energy expenditures, say even 5 miles of jogging, people are still susceptible to 20-pound variations, or even more, as a function of the amount of fat in their diets.

About 95 percent of the persons who have any weight to lose will lose it by cutting the fat in their diets to the following levels:

Women   20 to 40 grams a day
Men   30 to 60 grams a day

And, if they are in a sedentary occupation, they'll lose weight by increasing physical activity to the tune of between 200 and 300 calories of extra energy expenditure every day. This can be accomplished with about forty-five to sixty minutes of brisk walking, or any other equivalent exercise.

What about the other 5 percent for whom this nice combination of sound nutrition and exercise doesn't work? And what if that 5 percent includes you!

Then, in all likelihood, your carbohydrate intake is more than your particular metabolism can burn off, in spite of a healthful amount of physical activity and a low-fat diet. But let's start by assuming you fit in with the majority because the way to deal with your diet in this case is quite simple and painless. There is no need to take drastic steps until they prove to be necessary. If, unfortunately, you find that the simple approach is not effective, I'll show you what additional steps you need to take later in this chapter.

It's essential that you put my recommendations for physical activity in practice. Go all the way! Although it's possible for most people to lose a significant amount of weight just by cutting the fat in their diets to between 20 and 25 percent of total calories, with only a small increase in activity, my experience is that they get about halfway to the weight they'd like to be and hit a plateau. That is all the adjustment that their bodies will make to a 20 to 25 percent fat diet if they remain sedentary. They are stuck there. To lose any more weight without adding forty-five to sixty minutes a day of activity can require cutting fat to as low as 10 percent of total calories.

A healthful diet can be designed with only 10 percent of calories from fat, and all overweight persons who do not suffer from a serious genetic defect will, in time, lose all their surplus body fat and become quite thin if they eat no more than 10 percent of their calories from fat. In addition, in some cases a diet this low in fat can stop the progression of atherosclerosis and possibly lead to a small reversal in persons who suffer from this disease. Most people, however, will find such a spartan diet a great bother to prepare and almost impossible to live with. Very few can remain motivated to do so, even in the presence of a life-threatening illness.[1]

But, as you will see below, it is very easy to design and prepare a palatable diet that contains between 20 and 25

[1]There are actually some people with a rare form of hyperlipidemia (elevated triglycerides in their bloodstream) who cannot tolerate a diet this low in fat together with 70 to 80 percent of calories from carbohydrate. You should not undertake this extreme form of diet without consultation with your physician.

percent of calories from fat. Together with the physical activity I recommend, almost all people will lose weight on such a diet. The low end of the target ranges that I suggest (20–40 grams of fat per day for women, 30–60 grams of fat for men) will tend to bring your diet down to around the 20 percent level in calories from fat, and will bring your weight down quickly. Once you have lost the weight you need to lose, you can begin to add a little more fat if you choose. But women do not need to go above 50 grams of fat per day to maintain their weight, or men 60. If you are very active and need extra calories, it's far healthier to get them from carbohydrate foods (fruit, vegetables, and grains) rather than from fat.

One of the nicest things about using the fat-gram approach to managing your weight is that once you learn where the fat is in your foods and find substitutes for high-fat foods that you can live with, there is no further need to count anything in your effort to maintain desirable weight— not calories and not fat grams. Just keep on eating the low-fat diet that you design over these next few weeks, and you are done with any need to keep track of what you are eating.

THE FOURTEEN-DAY MENU PLAN

Begin by keeping track of your fat intake using the Fat and Carbohydrate Counter in Appendix C. Use the Fourteen-Day Eating Record at the end of this chapter to monitor your intake over the next two weeks.

The fourteen sample daily menus below usually contain, on the average, about 25 grams of fat, between 210 and 250 grams of carbohydrate, and between 1300 and 1400 calories. If you use these menus, check with Appendix C for the precise nutritional values to enter on the eating chart.

I have intentionally held the fat content of my daily menus down to around 25 grams, to leave room for up to a tablespoon of added fat each day, which you can use as spread or in food preparation without exceeding the upper boundaries of the daily fat-gram goals that I have recommended. Add this fat with caution, however, since some people cannot lose weight very efficiently with this much added fat in their diets.

These menus are appropriate for women just as they stand and, together with forty-five to sixty minutes of daily activity, will lead to an average weight loss of between ½ and 1 pound per week. Men may increase the quantities suggested for main dishes at each meal by 50 percent (but do not increase the size of desserts and snacks).

Please resist trying to lose weight more quickly. If you have ever used a quick weight-loss program you must certainly be aware of the difficulty you faced afterward in trying to maintain your weight loss. Your goal in this program is not simply to "go on a diet" and then go off it once you have lost weight. That's a recipe for failure. Your task is to find low-fat substitutions for high-fat foods that you can live with permanently, choosing them between 80 and 90 percent of the time for all your meals and snacks. You don't have to deny yourself completely—just reserve high-fat foods for special occasions, perhaps once or twice a week.

My menus are based on easily obtained foods that will provide you with a nutritious low-fat diet. You can and should, however, substitute foods based on seasonal availability or your own taste preferences. Make substitutions from the same food group (that is, one meat for another, one fruit for another) and stick with foods that have about the same fat content as my examples.[2] In this way the nutritional value of your own daily menus will approximate my examples. Use the Fat and Carbohydrate Counter in Appendix C to keep track.

If you wish to improvise your own daily menus, use the Food Pyramid shown here, and include the recommended number of servings of foods from the various food groups. By eating a variety of foods from within each group you will assure yourself of obtaining all the vitamins and minerals that your body needs. If you stay within the recommended fat-gram goal each day, your own menus will result in carbohydrate and calorie contents that are similar to my menus without your having to make any special effort. Fat is the key. Unless, for one reason or another (such as a food sensitivity), you eliminate from your diet one of the food groups represented in the Food Pyramid, the other nutrients fall into place when you cut the fat without your paying them any special attention.

Dishes in boldface type in the menus refer to recipes in Chapter 6, where you will find a number of low-fat ways to prepare most of the best-liked foods in the American diet: beef, poultry, fish, pasta, casseroles, stir-fries, and legumes.[3]

[2]If you wish to reduce or eliminate animal products, substitute foods such as legumes and grains that will give you equivalent protein from plant sources.

[3]For a complete course in delicious, low-fat food preparation, I recommend *The Low-Fat Good Food Cookbook* (1994), which I wrote with my daughter, Terri Katahn, and which is published by W. W. Norton & Company.

Food Guide Pyramid

A Guide to Daily Food Choices

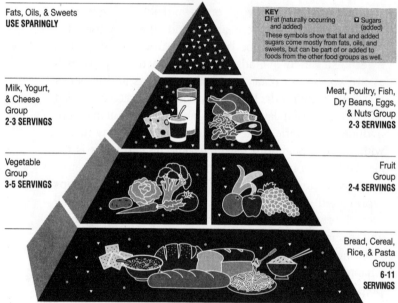

Fats, Oils, & Sweets
USE SPARINGLY

KEY
☐ Fat (naturally occurring and added)
☑ Sugars (added)
These symbols show that fat and added sugars come mostly from fats, oils, and sweets, but can be part of or added to foods from the other food groups as well.

Milk, Yogurt, & Cheese Group
2-3 SERVINGS

Meat, Poultry, Fish, Dry Beans, Eggs, & Nuts Group
2-3 SERVINGS

Vegetable Group
3-5 SERVINGS

Fruit Group
2-4 SERVINGS

Bread, Cereal, Rice, & Pasta Group
6-11 SERVINGS

SOURCE: U.S. Department of Agriculture/U.S. Department of Health and Human Services

MENUS

WEEK 1

Day 1

Breakfast
1 ounce raisin bran, 1 cup 1% milk, coffee or tea, 1 teaspoon
half-and-half

Mid-morning Snack
½ cup sliced fresh peaches

Lunch
Turkey sandwich (2 ounces breast meat, 2 slices whole-grain
bread, ¼ cup cranberry sauce, ¼ cup alfalfa sprouts), 1 ounce
pretzels, 1 cup 1% milk

Mid-afternoon Snack
1 orange

Dinner
Pasta (1 cup cooked) with **Red Clam Sauce**, 1½ cups dinner
salad,[4] 1 tablespoon low-fat dressing, 1 slice Italian bread,
1 **Chocolate-Chip Cookie**

Evening Snack
2 graham crackers

[4]Based on 1 cup romaine lettuce and ¼ cup each of shaved carrots and shredded
cabbage, plus a slice of tomato. Feel free to substitute the same total quantity of
your own favorite fresh vegetables. The nutritional value will remain similar.

DAY 2

BREAKFAST
Honey Bran Muffin, 1 cup 1% milk, coffee or tea, 1 teaspoon half-and-half

MID-MORNING SNACK
1 cup sliced fresh strawberries

LUNCH
½ cup canned refried beans, 2 corn tortillas, ⅓ cup each carrot sticks, celery sticks, and sliced radishes, 1 cup 1% milk

MID-AFTERNOON SNACK
½ cup seedless grapes

DINNER
1 serving **Marinated Flank Steak,** 1 medium baked potato, 1 cup green beans and water chestnuts, 1½ cups dinner salad, 1 tablespoon low-fat dressing, 1 cup orange and grapefruit sections

EVENING SNACK
4 cups air-popped popcorn

DAY 3

BREAKFAST
1 ounce shredded wheat, ½ cup fresh strawberries, 1 cup 1% milk, coffee or tea, 1 teaspoon half-and-half

MID-MORNING SNACK
1 banana

LUNCH
Chef salad (1½ cups dinner salad, 2 ounces lean ham, ½ ounce shredded cheese, ¼ cup croutons), 1 tablespoon low-fat dressing, 1 slice whole-grain bread, 1 cup 1% milk

MID-AFTERNOON SNACK
½ cup sliced pineapple

DINNER
1 serving **Baked Bass with Lemon-Wine Bouillon,** ½ baked
acorn squash with 1 teaspoon butter, 1 cup brussels sprouts,
1 cup fresh fruit salad, no-cal beverage

EVENING SNACK
1 slice cinnamon-raisin toast, 1 teaspoon jelly, 1 cup low-fat
yogurt

DAY 4

BREAKFAST
1 toasted bagel, 1 teaspoon jelly, 1 cup 1% milk, coffee or tea,
1 teaspoon half-and-half

MID-MORNING SNACK
1 medium apple

LUNCH
Turkey sandwich (2 ounces sliced turkey breast, 2 slices
whole-grain bread, 1 leaf romaine lettuce, 2 slices tomato,
2 teaspoons mustard), 1 cup orange and grapefruit sections,
no-cal beverage

MID-AFTERNOON SNACK
1 ounce flatbread

DINNER
½ cup **Indian Spiced Beans,** ½ cup brown rice, ½ cup spinach,
1 **New England Corn Muffin,** 1½ cups dinner salad,
1 tablespoon low-fat dressing, no-cal beverage

EVENING SNACK
4 cups air-popped popcorn

DAY 5

BREAKFAST
1 egg (or egg substitute) cooked without fat, 1 slice whole-grain toast, 1 teaspoon jelly, 1 cup 1% milk, coffee or tea, 1 teaspoon half-and-half

MID-MORNING SNACK
½ grapefruit

LUNCH
1 cup broth-based soup, ½ sandwich (1 slice whole-wheat bread, 1 ounce lean ham, 1 leaf romaine lettuce, 1 slice tomato, 1 teaspoon mustard), ⅓ cup carrot sticks, 1 cup 1% milk

MID-AFTERNOON SNACK
½ cup grapes

DINNER
1 serving **Oven-Fried Chicken**, 1 medium baked potato with 1 teaspoon butter, ½ cup summer squash, 1½ cups dinner salad, 1 tablespoon low-fat dressing, 1 slice whole-grain bread, no-cal beverage

EVENING SNACK
1 cup fresh strawberries

DAY 6

BREAKFAST
1 ounce bran flakes, ½ sliced banana, 1 cup 1% milk, coffee or tea, 1 teaspoon half-and-half

MID-MORNING SNACK
4 ounces grapefruit juice

LUNCH

1 cup broth-based vegetable soup, 1 **New England Corn Muffin**,
1 peach, no-cal beverage

MID-AFTERNOON SNACK

2 rice or popcorn cakes

DINNER

3 ounces lean, well-trimmed pork loin, 1 medium sweet potato,
1½ cups tossed salad, 1 tablespoon low-fat dressing, 1 slice
whole-grain bread

EVENING SNACK

½ cup frozen low-fat yogurt

DAY 7

BREAKFAST

¾ cup oatmeal with 1 tablespoon raisins, ¼ teaspoon cinnamon,
1 teaspoon light brown sugar, 1 cup 1% milk, coffee or tea,
1 teaspoon half-and-half

MID-MORNING SNACK

⅛th honeydew melon

LUNCH

Tuna salad (3 ounces canned white-meat tuna packed in water,
2 teaspoons low-fat mayonnaise, 1 teaspoon white wine
Worcestershire, 1 small stalk celery chopped, 1 scallion chopped,
3 leaves romaine lettuce, 2 slices tomato), 2 slices whole-grain
bread, no-cal beverage

MID-AFTERNOON SNACK

½ cup frozen low-fat yogurt

DINNER
1 serving **Japanese Beef Stir-Fry**, ½ cup brown rice, 1½ cups dinner salad, 1 tablespoon low-fat dressing, 1 two-inch-diameter whole-grain roll, 1 cup fresh fruit salad, no-cal beverage

EVENING SNACK
1 ounce raisin bran, 1 cup 1% milk

WEEK 2

DAY 8

BREAKFAST
2 slices French toast (2 slices French bread, soaked in mixture of ¼ cup egg substitute, ¼ cup 1% milk, pinch of salt), 1 ounce pancake syrup, coffee or tea, 1 teaspoon half-and-half

MID-MORNING SNACK
1 nectarine

LUNCH
1 cup vegetable soup, 1 ounce breadsticks, ⅓ cup each carrot sticks, celery sticks, and radishes, ½ cup fresh peaches, no-cal beverage

MID-AFTERNOON SNACK
1 ounce bagel chips

DINNER
1 serving **Chicken Divan**, ½ cup brown rice, ½ cup steamed broccoli, 1 two-inch-diameter dinner roll, $\frac{1}{12}$th angel food cake, 2 tablespoons fudge topping, 1 cup 1% milk

EVENING SNACK
½ cup fresh fruit salad

DAY 9

BREAKFAST
1 ounce Cheerios, ½ sliced banana, 1 cup 1% milk, coffee or tea,
1 teaspoon half-and-half

MID-MORNING SNACK
2 plums

LUNCH
Salmon salad (2 ounces canned salmon, 2 teaspoons low-fat
mayonnaise, 1 teaspoon white wine Worcestershire, 1 small stalk
celery chopped, 1 scallion chopped, 3 leaves romaine lettuce,
2 slices tomato, ¼ cup alfalfa sprouts), 1 bagel, 1 cup 1% milk

MID-AFTERNOON SNACK
½ cup frozen yogurt

DINNER
1 serving **Lemon-Pepper Beef**, 1 cup cooked pasta, 1 cup
brussels sprouts, 1 slice whole-grain bread, 1 ½ cups dinner
salad, 1 tablespoon low-fat dressing, no-cal beverage

EVENING SNACK
1 cup orange and grapefruit sections

DAY 10

BREAKFAST
1 serving (3) Hungry Jack pancakes (or other mix), 1 ounce
pancake syrup, 1 cup 1% milk, coffee or tea, 1 teaspoon
half-and-half

MID-MORNING SNACK
1 tangerine

LUNCH
Chef salad (1½ cups dinner salad, 2 ounces white-meat turkey, ½ ounce shredded cheese, ¼ cup croutons), 1 tablespoon low-fat dressing, 1 slice whole-grain bread, 1 cup 1% milk

MID-AFTERNOON SNACK
½ cup frozen yogurt

DINNER
1 serving **Fish Florentine**, ½ cup steamed carrots, ½ cup wild rice, 1 two-inch-diameter whole-grain roll, no-cal beverage

EVENING SNACK
½ cup sliced fresh strawberries

DAY 11

BREAKFAST
¾ cup oatmeal with 1 tablespoon raisins, ¼ teaspoon cinnamon, 1 teaspoon light brown sugar, 1 cup 1% milk, coffee or tea, 1 teaspoon half-and-half

MID-MORNING SNACK
1 banana

LUNCH
Tuna-stuffed tomato (3 ounces canned water-packed tuna, 2 teaspoons low-fat mayonnaise, 1 teaspoon white wine Worcestershire, 1 small stalk celery chopped, 1 large hollowed-out tomato), 1 serving flatbread, 1 cup 1% milk

MID-AFTERNOON SNACK
1 orange

DINNER
1 serving **Turkey Chop Suey**, 1 two-inch-diameter whole-grain roll, 1½ cups dinner salad, 1 tablespoon low-fat dressing, no-cal beverage

EVENING SNACK
1 cup plain nonfat yogurt, ½ cup berries

DAY 12

BREAKFAST
2 slices cinnamon-raisin toast, 1 teaspoon jelly, 1 cup 1% milk,
coffee or tea, 1 teaspoon half-and-half

MID-MORNING SNACK
½ grapefruit

LUNCH
Spinach salad (1 cup chopped spinach leaves, ¼ cup sliced
mushrooms, 2 slices Bermuda onion, ½ hard-boiled egg,
½ ounce shredded part-skim white cheese), 1 tablespoon low-fat
dressing, 1 slice whole-grain toast, no-cal beverage

MID-AFTERNOON SNACK
½ cup frozen yogurt

DINNER
1 serving **Vegetarian Chili Texas Style**, ½ cup brown rice, 1 cup
asparagus, 1 slice whole-wheat bread, no-cal beverage

EVENING SNACK
1 cup orange and grapefruit sections

DAY 13

BREAKFAST
1 ounce raisin bran, 1 cup 1% milk, coffee or tea, 1 teaspoon
half-and-half

MID-MORNING SNACK
⅛th honeydew melon

Lunch

Medium baked potato (topped with ½ cup low-fat cottage cheese, 1 scallion diced, ¼ cup sweet green peppers diced, Cajun seasoning), ⅓ cup carrot sticks, no-cal beverage

Mid-afternoon Snack

1 orange

Dinner

1 serving **Chicken Cacciatore**, 1 cup green beans, 1½ cups dinner salad, 1 tablespoon low-fat dressing, 1/12th angel food cake, 2 tablespoons fudge topping, 1 cup 1% milk

Evening Snack

½ cup berries

Day 14

Breakfast

¾ cup oatmeal with 1 tablespoon raisins, ¼ teaspoon cinnamon, 1 teaspoon light brown sugar, 1 cup 1% milk, coffee or tea, 1 teaspoon half-and-half

Mid-morning Snack

1 banana

Lunch

1 cup vegetable soup, 1 **New England Corn Muffin**, no-cal beverage

Mid-afternoon Snack

½ cup frozen yogurt

Dinner

1 serving **Spinach Lasagna**, 1 two-inch-diameter whole-grain roll, 1½ cups dinner salad, 1 tablespoon low-fat dressing, no-cal beverage

EVENING SNACK
1 cup orange and grapefruit sections

WHAT IF THE DIET AND ACTIVITY PROGRAM DOES NOT SEEM TO BE WORKING FOR YOU?

If the simple approach that I have just outlined does not seem to be working, you must first make sure you are really doing what I have asked you to do!

Research shows that almost everyone, including trained dietitians, underestimates their fat intake by 10 to 20 grams a day. Fat is well hidden in foods, especially in animal and dairy products, desserts, and snacks. Even identical foods labeled low-fat and lean, but produced by different manufacturers, can vary by several grams of fat in portions of identical size. Ask yourself:

Am I certain of the fat content of the processed foods and animal and dairy products that I am eating?

Am I keeping track of everything I eat?

Have I recorded the portions accurately?

When I use any added fat, do I know what a *level* teaspoon or tablespoon of fat, oil, or salad dressing looks like, so that I can be certain I am not underestimating added fat?

When you are certain that your fat intake is being accurately represented in your records, and you still have difficulty managing your weight, then it's time to take a look at carbohydrates.

From previous discussions you already know that, in weight-stable persons, the body converts almost no carbohydrate to fat. Small daily variations in carbohydrate consumption lead only to changes in glucose and water stores. Together with variations in your sodium intake, variation in carbohydrate consumption is one of the main dietary factors that leads to daily weight fluctuations that can amount to several pounds. With fat, however, 97 percent of excess fat calories at any given meal will go directly to your fat cells.

However, you cannot overdo carbohydrates continually without forcing your body to convert more and more of the carbohydrate calories to fat. For example, if you continually outeat your energy needs for a week, your body will gradually work up from about a 4 percent conversion of excess carbohydrate to fat to about 75 percent.

Some people have actually made the mistake of believing that once they have their fat content down to the level I recommend, they can eat anything they want, as long as it has little or no fat. So (and these are actual reports in my files) they have added to their daily diets two extra loaves of bread, or two family-size bags of pretzels, or six packages of jelly beans. This amounts to between 200 and 400 extra grams of carbohydrate and 1000 to 2000 extra calories. You can't do this on a daily basis and expect to lose weight!

If bringing your fat intake into the range I have set for you does not seem to be working, begin by setting the following carbohydrate limit as your starting point:

Women   250 grams carbohydrate per day
Men   300 grams carbohydrate per day

Keep track of your daily intake of carbohydrate together with fat in grams. Use the Fat and Carbohydrate Counter in Appendix C.

Women should keep their daily fat consumption to 20–25 grams, and men 30–35 grams. If the carbohydrate intake I've just recommended does not lead to weight loss, begin to decrease carbohydrates. Women may go as low as 200 grams and men to 250 grams per day. If you eat a wide variety of foods from each of the food groups (use the Food Pyramid shown earlier in this chapter), you will still be consuming a nutritious diet.

If you are certain your eating record is accurate, and my recommendations still do not work in spite of your meeting a *daily* activity goal of *at least* forty-five minutes of walking (or its equivalent), I suggest that you consult either your physician or a registered dietitian for help. Something is wrong that requires personal, professional supervision.

FOURTEEN-DAY EATING RECORD

Column headings: FAT = FAT; CARB = CARBOHYDRATE; CAL = CALORIES. List the foods you eat at all meals and for snacks. Look up the fat and carbohydrate grams, and the calories, in the Fat and Carbohydrate Counter in Appendix C. Keep this record for the next fourteen days. Make additional copies to continue for more than

	DAY 1			DAY 2			DAY 3		
DATE BEGUN:	FAT	CARB	CAL	FAT	CARB	CAL	FAT	CARB	CAL
BREAKFAST									
SNACK									
LUNCH									
SNACK									
DINNER									
SNACK									
TOTAL									

fourteen days. Continue to keep a record for at least three weeks if you have just quit smoking.

Fat-gram targets: Women   20–40 grams per day
                   Men   30–60 grams per day

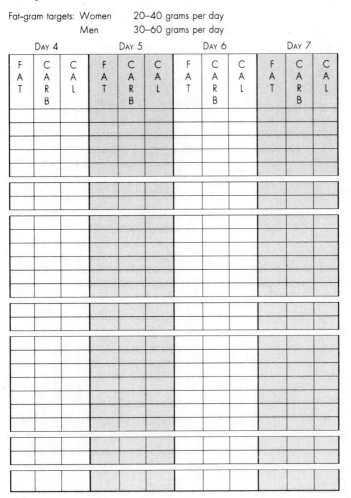

DAY 4			DAY 5			DAY 6			DAY 7		
F A T	C A R B	C A L	F A T	C A R B	C A L	F A T	C A R B	C A L	F A T	C A R B	C A L

FOURTEEN-DAY EATING RECORD *(continued)*

	Day 8			Day 9			Day 10		
	F A T	C A R B	C A L	F A T	C A R B	C A L	F A T	C A R B	C A L
BREAKFAST									
SNACK									
LUNCH									
SNACK									
DINNER									
SNACK									
TOTAL									

Day 11			Day 12			Day 13			Day 14		
F A T	C A R B	C A L	F A T	C A R B	C A L	F A T	C A R B	C A L	F A T	C A R B	C A L

6

RECIPES

The recipes that follow illustrate some basic ways to prepare a number of favorite dishes. Pay attention to the basic ingredients, especially the amount of added fat, which is always kept to a minimum consistent with good taste. Adapt your own favorite recipes for fish, poultry, meat, casseroles, and so on, using the suggestions for food preparation for the dinner meal in Table 3 of Chapter 3, and your recipes will be similar to mine in their fat, carbohydrate, and calorie values.

BAKED BASS WITH LEMON-WINE BOUILLON

4 bass fillets, about 1 pound raw
½ teaspoon dried chives
¼ teaspoon dried chervil OR dried parsley
¼ teaspoon dried tarragon
1 tablespoon lemon juice (fresh is best!)
½ cup dry white wine
½ cup bread crumbs
1 tablespoon butter OR margarine

1. Place the fillets in a shallow baking dish. Sprinkle with seasonings and lemon juice. Pour the wine over the fish.
2. Bake at 400 degrees for 15 minutes. Then sprinkle the bread crumbs on top, and dot with butter. Bake 15 minutes more, or until fish flakes easily with a fork.

4 servings of 3½ ounces each (cooked weight)

Per serving: **7 g fat**, 10 g carbohydrate, 209 calories, 75 mg cholesterol, 1 g dietary fiber, 208 mg sodium

FISH FLORENTINE

This Italian style of cooking (with spinach) works as well with veal and chicken.

1 pound fish fillets (flounder or sole)
1 package (10 ounces) frozen chopped spinach, thawed and drained

10 *whole-wheat crackers, crushed*
 2 *tablespoons wheat germ*
 3 *tablespoons Parmesan* OR *sapsago cheese*

1. Arrange the fillets in the bottom of a shallow baking dish.
2. Cover the fish with the well-drained spinach.
3. Combine the cracker crumbs, wheat germ, and cheese, and pour over the fish and spinach.
4. Bake, uncovered, at 400 degrees for 15 to 20 minutes.

4 servings of 3 ounces each (cooked weight), plus spinach

Per serving: **4 g fat**, 9 g carbohydrate, 181 calories, 62 mg cholesterol, 2 g dietary fiber, 296 mg sodium

CHICKEN DIVAN

 6 *chicken breasts, boned and skinned, 5 ounces each*
1½ *cups chicken stock*
 4 *tablespoons whole-wheat flour*
 ¾ *cup skim* OR *low-fat milk*
 ¼ *cup nonfat dry milk*
 ¼ *cup white wine*
 ¼ *teaspoon pepper*
 1 *large bunch fresh broccoli* OR *2 packages (10 ounces each) frozen broccoli spears*
 ½ *cup sapsago cheese* OR *Parmesan, grated*
 1 *tablespoon fresh parsley, chopped*

1. Wrap the chicken breasts in aluminum foil and bake at 350 degrees for 30 minutes.
2. Meanwhile, bring the chicken stock to a boil.
3. In another pan over low heat, combine ¼ cup of the boiling broth and the flour. Cook and stir until smooth. Gradually add the rest of the broth, stirring until thickened. Remove from heat.
4. Combine the skim and nonfat dry milk, and add to the broth, along with the wine and pepper.
5. Place the broccoli spears in a shallow baking dish. Top with half the sauce. Arrange the cooked chicken breasts on top of the broccoli. Combine half the cheese with the rest of the sauce, and pour over the chicken. Sprinkle with parsley and the remaining cheese, and bake at 350 degrees for 20 minutes.

6 servings of 1 breast, plus vegetables

Per serving: **6 g fat**, 12 g carbohydrate, 260 calories, 81 mg cholesterol, 3 g dietary fiber, 292 mg sodium

CHICKEN CACCIATORE

1 small onion, chopped
1 clove garlic, minced (or ½ teaspoon garlic powder)
⅓ cup water
1 14½-ounce can whole tomatoes, chopped
1 6-ounce can tomato paste
1 teaspoon oregano
Salt and fresh-ground black pepper to taste

4 chicken breasts, skinless and boneless
4 cups hot cooked spaghetti or rice

1. In a skillet over medium heat, cook onion and garlic with water, covered, for 5 minutes or until onion is tender.
2. Stir in the tomatoes, tomato paste, and seasonings. Reduce heat, cover and simmer for 10–15 minutes.
3. Add the chicken and cook, covered, for 30 minutes. Uncover and cook another 15 minutes.
4. Serve over spaghetti or rice.

4 servings

Per serving with 1 cup spaghetti: **5 g fat**, 54 g carbohydrate, 402 calories, 73 mg cholesterol, 6 g dietary fiber, 394 mg sodium

OVEN-FRIED CHICKEN

1 tablespoon vegetable oil
1 teaspoon lemon juice
3 pounds chicken pieces, skinned
About ⅓ cup skim OR low-fat milk OR buttermilk
½ cup flour (all-purpose, whole-wheat, or combination)
1½ teaspoons paprika
¼ teaspoon salt
¼ teaspoon black pepper
¼ teaspoon onion powder
¼ teaspoon garlic powder
⅛ teaspoon cayenne pepper

¼ teaspoon marjoram
¼ teaspoon oregano

1. Combine the oil and lemon juice, and brush each piece of skinned chicken with the mixture.
2. Place the milk in a shallow bowl, and set aside. Combine the flour(s) and seasonings in another bowl, mixing well.
3. Dip the chicken into the milk, coating all sides. Then coat with the flour mixture.
4. Place the chicken "skin" side down in a foil-covered baking pan. Cover loosely with foil, and bake at 350 degrees for 30 minutes. Turn the chicken pieces over, and bake 30 minutes more, or until cooked through.

6 servings of 3½ ounces each (cooked weight)

Per serving: **7 g fat**, 9 g carbohydrate, 233 calories, 89 mg cholesterol, 1 g dietary fiber, 180 mg sodium

TURKEY CHOP SUEY

1 pound lean ground turkey
1 can (16 ounces) bean sprouts, drained
1 cup chopped celery
½ cup chopped onion
1 can (8 ounces) water chestnuts, drained and sliced
1 can (5 ounces) sliced mushrooms, drained
¼ teaspoon ground ginger
1 can (10½ ounces) condensed beef or chicken broth
2 tablespoons soy sauce
2 tablespoons cornstarch (or ¼ cup flour)
3 cups cooked brown rice

1. In a large skillet, brown the ground turkey. Drain off any fat.
2. Add the vegetables, ginger, and all but ¼ cup of the broth. Bring to a boil over medium-high heat. Reduce heat, cover, and simmer for 20 minutes.
3. Combine the ¼ cup of reserved broth with the soy sauce and cornstarch. Add to the meat and vegetable mixture, stirring until thickened and bubbly. Serve over the rice.

6 servings

Per serving: **7 g fat**, 34 g carbohydrate, 309 calories, 64 mg cholesterol, 4 g dietary fiber, 693 mg sodium

LEMON-PEPPER BEEF

1 pound lean top round steak, well trimmed
¼ cup dry red wine
2 to 3 tablespoons lemon juice
½ teaspoon salt
1 bay leaf
2 yellow or red sweet peppers, cut in eighths
Fresh-ground black pepper to taste

1. Combine all ingredients in a large bowl or pan and marinate overnight, or at least 6 hours, in the refrigerator. Turn beef and peppers occasionally.
2. Place beef on broiler pan about 4 inches from heat and broil about 8 minutes. Turn, and add the pepper pieces

to the pan. After 6 minutes or so, turn the peppers over, then broil about 4 minutes more for medium-well-done beef. Slice the beef thinly across the grain, and serve with the peppers.

4 servings of 3 ounces each (cooked weight)

Per serving: **4 g fat**, 4 g carbohydrate, 177 calories, 71 mg cholesterol, 1 g dietary fiber, 320 mg sodium

MARINATED FLANK STEAK

1 pound lean flank steak
¼ cup chopped green onions
2 cloves garlic
2 tablespoons soy sauce
1 tablespoon red wine
1 tablespoon water
1 teaspoon olive oil

Combine all ingredients in a large bowl or pan and marinate for at least 4 hours (preferably overnight) in the refrigerator. Use marinade for basting while broiling or cooking.

Variation: Mince a 1-inch piece of fresh ginger (peeled) and add to the marinade for an Oriental flavor.

4 servings of 3 ounces each (cooked weight)

Per serving: **10 g fat**, 1 g carbohydrate, 194 calories, 57 mg cholesterol, 0 dietary fiber, 477 mg sodium

JAPANESE BEEF STIR-FRY

4 beef tenderloin steaks (about 4 ounces each)
1 tablespoon peanut oil
2 packages (6 ounces each) frozen pea pods, thawed
¼ head red cabbage, thinly sliced
¼ inch fresh gingerroot, minced, OR ground ginger to taste
1 tablespoon saké (optional)
Dash tamari sauce OR soy sauce

1. Heat a wok or heavy skillet over medium-high heat for several minutes. Meanwhile, trim the beef of all visible fat and slice the beef into thin slices.
2. Add the oil to the pan, then the beef. Cook, stirring constantly, until browned.
3. Lower the heat to medium, remove the meat from the pan, and set aside.
4. Add the pea pods, cabbage, and gingerroot to the wok, and cook for 5 minutes, stirring constantly.
5. Return the meat to the wok, and stir in the saké and the soy sauce. Cover, and let simmer for a few more minutes, until the vegetables are just tender and the meat is cooked the way you like it.

4 servings of 3 ounces each (cooked weight), plus vegetables

Per serving: **12 g fat**, 9 g carbohydrate, 260 calories, 71 mg cholesterol, 3 g dietary fiber, 81 mg sodium

SPINACH LASAGNA

½ *pound lasagna noodles, preferably whole wheat*
1 *medium onion, chopped*
2 *cloves garlic, minced*
1 *tablespoon olive oil*
Water as needed
1 *pound 1% low-fat cottage cheese*
¼ *cup grated Parmesan*
1½ *pounds fresh spinach, chopped and packed (about 2*
   cups), or 1 10-ounce package frozen chopped spinach,
   thawed and drained
2 *egg whites, beaten*
¼ *teaspoon fresh-ground black pepper*
2 *to 3 tablespoons fresh parsley, chopped*
Nonstick cooking spray
6 *cups tomato or meatless spaghetti sauce*
6 *ounces part-skim mozzarella, grated*

1. Cook the lasagna noodles according to package directions.
2. While the noodles are cooking, sauté the onion and garlic in the olive oil, adding a tablespoon or two of water as needed to keep from sticking.
3. Combine the cottage cheese, Parmesan, spinach, egg whites, black pepper, parsley, and sautéed onion and garlic, mixing well.
4. Spray a 9 × 13 × 2-inch casserole dish with nonstick cooking spray. Spread ¼ of the tomato or spaghetti sauce over the bottom and then arrange a layer of noo-

dles, top with ⅓ of the cheese-spinach mixture, sprinkle with ⅓ of the mozzarella, and top with tomato sauce. Repeat layers twice more, ending with sauce.

5. Cover pan with aluminum foil, crimping edges tightly. Bake at 350 degrees for 40 minutes; remove foil and bake 10–15 minutes more.

12 servings

Per serving: **5 g fat**, 28 g carbohydrate, 213 calories, 12 mg cholesterol, 4 g dietary fiber, 903 mg sodium

RED CLAM SAUCE

2 cups chopped onions
1 large green pepper, chopped
8 cloves garlic, minced
12 ounces mushrooms, sliced
2 tablespoons olive oil
2 tablespoons water
4 6½-ounce cans minced clams, with liquid
1 teaspoon dried basil
2 dried red peppers (hot) OR ½ teaspoon crushed hot red pepper
¼ teaspoon fresh-ground black pepper
1 15-ounce can tomato sauce
1 6-ounce can tomato paste

1. In a 4-quart covered saucepan, sauté onions, green pepper, garlic, and mushrooms in olive oil and water over medium-low heat until onions are translucent.

2. Add remaining ingredients and simmer, covered, over low heat for 45 minutes.

10 servings of 1 cup each

Per serving: **4 g fat**, 15 g carbohydrate, 140 calories, 26 mg cholesterol, 3 g dietary fiber, 38 mg sodium *Add per cup of pasta:* **1 g fat**, 4 g carbohydrate, 159 calories, 0 cholesterol, 1 g dietary fiber, 1 mg sodium

INDIAN SPICED BEANS

2 cups dried red or kidney beans
4 cups stock
1 medium onion, sliced
1 medium tomato, chopped
1 clove garlic, chopped
2 dried red peppers
1 bay leaf
¼ teaspoon fresh-ground black pepper
¼ teaspoon ground cloves

Wash beans and remove any stones. Place all ingredients in a 4-quart saucepan. Bring to a boil and reduce heat. Cover and cook for 4 hours on low heat.

6 servings of ¾ cup each

Per serving: **2 g fat**, 42 g carbohydrate, 248 calories, 0 cholesterol, 14 g dietary fiber, 230 mg sodium

VEGETARIAN CHILI TEXAS STYLE

1 cup chopped onions (2 medium-size onions)
4 cloves garlic, minced
2 cups vegetable stock (or use vegetable bouillon)
1 15-ounce can whole tomatoes, cut up, with juice
1 6-ounce can tomato paste
3 tablespoons chili powder
1 teaspoon vinegar (cider or red wine)
1 teaspoon ground cumin
½ teaspoon ground coriander
½ teaspoon oregano
¼ teaspoon fresh-ground black pepper
3 whole dried red peppers (hot)
2 16-ounce cans red or kidney beans, drained

1. In a 4-quart saucepan, simmer the onions and garlic in 3 tablespoons of the stock until translucent.
2. Add all remaining ingredients except the beans and simmer for 45 minutes.
3. Add beans and simmer another 15 minutes.

8 servings of 1 cup each

Per serving: **1 g fat**, 34 g carbohydrate, 179 calories, 0 cholesterol, 12 g dietary fiber, 622 mg sodium

HONEY BRAN MUFFINS

   2 cups 100% bran cereal
   ⅓ cup honey
1¼ cups skim milk
   1 egg
   1 cup all-purpose flour
   1 teaspoon baking soda
   ½ teaspoon salt

1. Combine the cereal, honey, and milk, and let stand for 2 minutes. Add the egg, beating well.
2. Stir together the flour, baking soda, and salt; add to the cereal mixture, stirring *only until combined*. Portion the batter evenly into lightly greased 2½-inch muffin-pan cups.
3. Bake at 400 degrees for 25 minutes or until a toothpick inserted in the center of a muffin comes out clean. Let stand about 5 minutes before removing from the pan. Serve immediately.

12 muffins

Per muffin: **1 g fat**, 28 g carbohydrate, 117 calories, 16 mg cholesterol, 5 g dietary fiber, 337 mg sodium

NEW ENGLAND CORN MUFFINS

   ½ cup honey
   1 cup Egg Beaters
1¾ cups skim milk

¼ *cup vegetable oil*
⅓ *cup sugar*
 2 *tablespoons baking powder*
3½ *cups all-purpose flour*
 1 *cup yellow cornmeal*
 ¼ *teaspoon salt*
Nonstick vegetable cooking spray (optional)

1. In a large bowl, whisk together the honey, Egg Beaters, milk, and oil.
2. Add the dry ingredients and mix with an electric mixer at medium-high speed for 2 minutes.
3. Spray two muffin tins with cooking spray or line with baking cups. Fill each cup ¾ full. Bake at 400 degrees for about 15 minutes, or until tops are golden brown.

24 muffins

Per muffin: **3 g fat**, 25 g carbohydrate, 145 calories, 0 cholesterol, 1 g dietary fiber, 104 mg sodium

CHOCOLATE-CHIP COOKIES

½ *cup butter, softened*
½ *cup brown sugar, firmly packed*
½ *cup granulated white sugar*
 1 *teaspoon vanilla*
 1 *teaspoon water*
½ *cup Egg Beaters*

1 *cup whole-wheat flour*
1 *cup all-purpose flour*
1 *teaspoon baking soda*
1 *teaspoon salt*
6 *ounces semisweet chocolate chips*
½ *cup chopped nuts*

1. Preheat the oven to 375 degrees.
2. In a large bowl, combine the butter, sugars, vanilla, and water. Beat in the egg substitute.
3. In another bowl, combine the flours, baking soda, and salt. Gradually add this to the wet ingredients, blending well. Stir in the chocolate chips and the nuts.
4. Drop by rounded teaspoonful onto Teflon or ungreased baking sheets. Bake until golden brown, about 8 to 10 minutes.

Variation: Add a couple of teaspoons of grated orange rind to the batter before baking, for Orange Chocolate-Chip Cookies.

3 dozen cookies, about 2 inches in diameter

Per cookie: **5 g fat**, 13 g carbohydrate, 99 calories, 7 mg cholesterol, 1 g dietary fiber, 114 mg sodium

Appendix A

Strength-Training Routine

Strength training builds muscles. Because muscle cells are more active around the clock than fat cells, building muscles increases your resting metabolic rate. This will help combat the metabolic slowdown that occurs when you quit smoking. In addition, strength-training exercises burn a relatively high percentage of glucose in your fuel mixture, compared with fat. This can help burn off any excess carbohydrate that you may consume in an attempt to alleviate some of the symptoms that occur when you quit smoking.

It's generally best for women just starting a strength-training program to use 3-pound weights and for men to use 5-pound or 3-kilo (6.6-pound) weights. You can use books in place of weights. You can increase the weights by a few pounds as your strength increases. However, to avoid injury, it is generally best to increase the repetitions of the training movements rather than attempt to use very heavy weights.

The following set of exercises focuses on your upper body, legs, and stomach. You will find additional exercises in the booklet that comes with a set of weights. You can get excellent supervision in the development of a strength-training program at your local YMCA or YWCA.

Be sure to check with your physician before beginning any new fitness program.

UPPER BODY SERIES

1. *Two for the shoulders.* Hold arms at your sides with palms facing the rear. Keeping arms straight, raise weights forward to shoulder height and return to down position, slowly and with control. Breathe normally at all times. Work up to 10 repetitions, then rest for at least one deep breath. Then turn the weights so that your palms face your body, and raise your arms outward to the sides, up to shoulder level. Work up to 10 repetitions.

2. *Biceps curl.* Stand straight with arms at sides, palms facing forward. Curl forearms up to shoulder 10 times at a moderate pace.

3. *Triceps.* Keep elbows next to your body, bend forward at about a 60-degree angle from the hips, and curl forearms, bringing weights up to your shoulders. Then, keeping elbows next to your body, straighten your arms out in back behind you. Repeat until you feel some strain and stop. This will build the muscle on the back of your arms, and help reduce the likelihood of loose skin on your upper arms if you have been losing weight.

4. *Forward, up, and out.* Standing upright, start with arms

at your sides, palms facing body. Curling at the elbows, bring weights forward and up almost to the shoulders. Continuing in one uninterrupted motion, spread arms out to your sides, shoulder level, palms facing forward. Keep your arms slightly bent to avoid excessive strain. Return along the same path as you began and repeat up to 10 times.

LEG SERIES

5. *Heel lifts.* With weights at your side, go up and down slowly on your toes several times, resting about a second at the top each time.

6. *Half squats.* (If you are more than a few pounds overweight, don't use any extra weight for this exercise.) With arms at sides, feet at shoulder width, toes facing slightly out, squat down one-third to one-half of the way to the floor. Do not go beyond the point where your thighs are parallel to the floor, and keep your knees over your feet when squatting.

STOMACH SERIES

7. *Bent-knee sit-up.* Lie on your back with knees bent and feet close to your buttocks. Curl your head and shoulders about halfway up to your knees to begin with. (As you get stronger, try to get closer to your knees.) Roll back down. Arms can be held out in front of you to start, and then, as you get stronger, they can be folded across your chest. Ultimately, hands are held behind your head.

8. *Reverse sit-up*. Lying flat on the floor with arms at your sides, bring your heels back to your buttocks, and then lift knees to your chest, raising hips off the floor. Return to starting position and repeat several times. Breathe normally.

Finally, one of the very best strengthening exercises of all is the push-up, but it should not be undertaken until your stomach muscles are reasonably strong and until you can do a push-up resting on your knees rather than your toes. You can practice some easier versions of the push-up by pushing off against a wall until you get stronger.

Appendix B

Relaxation Training and Meditation

DEEP MUSCULAR RELAXATION

You can achieve both mental and physical relaxation with a technique called "deep muscular relaxation." It works because, with mentally focused training, tensed muscles can become more relaxed than they were prior to the tension. When deep muscular relaxation training is combined with the specific "breath of relaxation" that I will show you as you practice the complete technique, you can achieve almost instantaneous physical and mental relief. The technique has proven to be of great value to persons who face great tension and who need to be able to relax instantly in order to achieve maximum performance—basketball players at the foul line, biathalon athletes the moment before they shoot at their targets, and so on.

Training begins by tensing and relaxing various sets of muscles throughout your body. This will enable you to experience the relaxed state you are aiming for. After a few days of practice, you will no longer need to tense your muscles before relaxing them. You will simply use the "breath of relaxation" and let loose in any region of your body where you feel tension. At the same time you clear your mind for a few moments, and then make a new beginning at whatever you were doing.

You will need to set aside about twenty minutes each of the next few days for practice. You should be sitting in a comfortable chair (with or without arms) in a quiet place where you will not be disturbed. If your chair has no arms, rest your hands in your lap, except when the exercise calls for hand movements.

When you tense your muscles during training, go only to about three-quarters of their maximum tension. More is not needed. Do each exercise twice, relax for 5 or 10 seconds in between, then proceed to the next.

You can do these exercises with your eyes open or closed, but you will probably be more focused and relaxed afterward if you do them with your eyes closed. Remember to breathe normally throughout except in the special breathing exercise.

THE DEEP MUSCULAR RELAXATION
TRAINING ROUTINE

1. Make a fist with your right hand. Hold it for 5 seconds, focusing on the tension in the muscles in your hand and up your arm. Relax, and note the difference between the tension and the relaxation.

2. Make fists with both hands. Hold for 5 seconds, noting feelings in the muscles involved. Relax.

Always remember to focus on the difference in the feelings in your muscles as you do the tension part of the exercise, and contrast that with the feelings as you let go and relax. It helps to think "Let go" as you relax.

3. Make fists with both hands and slowly raise your forearms up to your shoulders, imagining that you are lifting fairly heavy weights. Hold for 5 seconds, then relax ("let go") and return your arms to the resting position.

The next seven exercises are for the head, neck, and shoulders, which are focal points for tension in most people.

4. Raise your eyebrows as far as you can. Hold for 5 seconds. Relax.

5. Crease your forehead (bringing your eyebrows together). Hold for 5 seconds. Relax.

6. Press your lips together. Hold for 5 seconds. Relax.

7. Scrunch up your whole face (make a "funny face"; it doesn't matter exactly how, just as long as you feel some tension in several muscle areas of your face). Hold for 5 seconds. Relax.

8. Lean your head to the right (without adding any special tension). Just note the naturally occurring tension on the sides of your neck as you do this. Hold for 5 seconds. Relax. Repeat the exercise leaning to the left. Then repeat leaning forward, bringing your chin toward your chest.

(Remember to keep breathing normally. And take your time—don't rush through these exercises!)

9. Raise your shoulders toward your ears (without adding any special tension). Hold for 5 seconds. Relax.

10. Shrug your shoulders; that is, bring them as far forward and toward each other in front of your chest as you can. Hold for 5 seconds. Relax.

The next exercise is the *breath of relaxation*.

11. Take a deep breath by first expanding your stomach area, then mid-chest, and finally upper chest so that your lungs are filled to their maximum. Note the tension that occurs naturally in your upper body. Hold your breath for a count of 5 and exhale, letting loose in your neck, shoulders, upper arms, and anywhere else that you noted any tension. Repeat this exercise with particular attention to "letting go" as you exhale.

You can practice this exercise by itself, several times a day. With just a small amount of practice you will be able to "let go" and relax any time you need to. Just take a deep breath, and consciously release tension in your upper body as you exhale. Besides being an almost instantaneous release of tension, it clears your mind for a few moments of mental relaxation.

The next three exercises are for your midsection.

12. Tense your stomach muscles as though to protect yourself from a blow to your midsection. Hold for 5 seconds. Relax.

13. Press your back against your chair. Hold for 5 seconds. Relax.

14. Squeeze your buttocks together. Hold for 5 seconds. Relax.

The next set of three exercises is for your lower body.

15. Press your knees together. Hold for 5 seconds. Relax.

16. Press your heels down against the floor. Hold for 5 seconds. Relax.

17. Pull your toes back toward the soles of your feet. Hold for 5 seconds. Relax.

Finish the entire relaxation training routine by repeating the breath of relaxation twice. Then let your attention focus on the feeling in various parts of your body. Start with your head and work down. If you feel any residual tension in any part of your body, give that part a little wiggle, and consciously "let go."

Sit quietly for a few moments, breathe normally, and then open your eyes if they have been closed. You are ready to resume your regular daily activities.

With a couple of days' practice the sense of how your body feels when it is relaxed will be in your mind and under mental control. You will no longer need to tense your muscles before directing them to relax. Just take a deep breath and let go in whatever part of your body you felt any tension as you exhale. If you are like most people, you probably experience a certain amount of tension in your head, neck, and shoulder regions, which, fortunately, are the regions most easily controlled and relaxed with the breath of relaxation exercise.

MEDITATION

Although there are a number of different forms of meditation, all focus on breathing and some relaxing mental procedure. Whichever specific way you choose can, with practice, have beneficial physical and mental effects, including the lowering of blood pressure, heart rate, respiration rate, as well as clearing of the mind.

Here is a simple but effective meditation technique that you can learn quickly and which I think will give you a great deal of satisfaction from the very first time you practice it.

Go to a quiet place where you can sit comfortably without being disturbed. Use an armchair if possible, so you can support your elbows and let your hands rest comfortably in your lap.

Close your eyes.

Check out your body.

If you feel any tension in your neck and shoulders, just rotate your head easily and slowly first in one direction, then the other, a couple of times. Wiggle your shoulders.

Focus on your breathing. Breathe slowly and naturally.

Quiet your mind by focusing in one of the following ways:

Pay attention only to the physical experience of breathing as you slowly inhale—that is, your chest expanding, the feeling of the air flowing in through your nostrils.

Make some sort of sound mentally, or repeat a word mentally, as you slowly exhale—for example, "uhmmmm," the word "one," or any other word, phrase, or prayer that, because of its meaning in your life, has a calming effect.

Should outside thoughts intrude, as they probably will, especially when you first begin to practice meditation, just pull back and distance yourself from them. Simply "notice them" as though they came from someplace outside yourself. It's very important to stay quiet and relaxed, and never to feel that anything you experience while meditating is somehow "wrong" or that you are not doing it "right." Even if you find yourself doing it many times, this act of putting yourself at a distance from any intrusion, becoming completely dispassionate no matter what your mind happens to do, and returning to your word or phrase and calm rhythmic breathing, is the key to experiencing the benefits of meditation.

If you spend about twenty minutes in meditation each day I think you will find that a feeling of calmness and of being in control will spread to other aspects of your life.

Here are some variations that you might enjoy in your meditation:

1. Count slowly to 4 as you breathe in and to a count of either 4 or 6 as you breathe out. Some people find it more relaxing to breathe out more slowly than in, but it's up to you to decide what feels best to you.

2. Instead of a word or counting as you breathe, just establish a calm rhythm, and simply "listen." Don't do anything but listen to all the sounds around you. Focus on your breathing and your ears. When thoughts intrude, as they will, do the distancing exercise and return to listening. This meditation approach involves different parts of the brain than when you repeat sounds to yourself (a word or phrase). I find this particularly relaxing.

3. "Meditation in motion is superior to meditation at rest," according to one Oriental teacher of meditation. If you can walk or jog in a safe place where you don't have to pay attention to traffic, dogs, or other distractions, get into a steady rhythm and count your steps as you breathe in and out (for example, 4 steps in, 4 steps out). Or simply switch into your "listening" mode and listen to what's going on around you. It's important with meditation in motion only that you have a rhythm to your motion. I have known runners and swimmers who go into an almost trancelike state during activity, but you have to be able to do the activity easily and without paying it any attention.

With meditation in motion you obtain the benefits of two activities—you burn many extra calories and end up being greatly relaxed.

APPENDIX C

FAT AND CARBOHYDRATE COUNTER

	Serving	Total Fat g.	% Cal. from fat	Carbs. in g.	Cal.
Beverages					
apple juice	6 fl. oz.	0	0	21.8	87
beer					
regular*	12 fl. oz.	0	0	13.2	146
light*	12 fl. oz.	0	0	4.8	100
nonalcoholic	12 fl. oz.	0	0	14.1	70
carbonated drink					
regular	12 fl. oz.	0	0	38.5	151
sugar free	12 fl. oz.	0	0	0.3	2
club soda/seltzer	12 fl. oz.	0	0	0	0
coffee, brewed or instant	8 fl. oz.	0	0	1	5
coffee, flavored mixes, instant	6 fl. oz.	2.4	52	6	55
cordials and liqueurs, 54 proof*	1 fl. oz.	0	0	16.3	116
daiquiri*	3.5 fl. oz.	0	0	7.2	194
eggnog, nonalcoholic, w/whole milk	8 fl. oz.	19.0	50	34.4	342
fruit punch	8 fl. oz.	0	0	29.4	116
Gatorade sports drink	8 fl. oz.	0	0	14.0	50
gin, 90 proof*	1 fl. oz.	0	0	0	73
grape juice drink, canned	6 fl. oz.	0	0	24.2	94
Kool-Aid, from mix, any flavor	8 fl. oz.	0	0	25.1	98
lemonade, mix or frzn	8 fl. oz.	0	0	26.9	102
lemonade, sugar-free	8 fl. oz.	0	0	1.3	5

*Although alcohol contains no fat, scientific evidence suggests that it may facilitate fat storage and hamper your weight-loss efforts. Excessive alcohol intake is detrimental to your health. We concur with other health organizations in recommending discretion in the use of alcoholic beverages.

	Serving	Total Fat g.	% Cal. from fat	Carbs. in g.	Cal.
orange juice, unsweetened	6 fl. oz.	0	0	19.1	83
pineapple–orange juice	6 fl. oz.	0	0	23	100
rum, 80 proof*	1 fl. oz.	0	0	0	65
Tang, orange or grape	8 fl. oz.	0	0	29.2	117
tea, brewed or instant	8 fl. oz.	0	0	0.4	2
tonic water	8 fl. oz.	0	0	21.4	83
vodka*	1 fl. oz.	0	0		65
whiskey*	1 fl. oz.	0	0	0.6	70
wine*					
dessert and apertif	4 fl. oz.	0	0	14.0	180
red or rosé	4 fl. oz.	0	0	0.9	85
white, dry or medium	4 fl. oz.	0	0	1.6	72
wine cooler	8 fl. oz.	0	0	2.0	143

Breads and Flours

	Serving	Total Fat g.	% Cal. from fat	Carbs. in g.	Cal.
bagel, cinnamon raisin	1 medium	2.0	8	48.0	240
bagel, plain	1 medium	1.4	8	30.9	163
biscuit					
baking powder	1 medium	5.0	45	12.0	100
buttermilk	1 medium	5.0	45	12.0	100
from mix	1 medium	3.0	27	15.0	100
Bisquick mix	1 cup	16.0	30	74.0	480
Boston brown bread					
canned	½-in. slice	0.6	6	18.0	85
w/raisins, canned	½-in. slice	0.6	6	18.0	88
bread					
cracked wheat	1 slice	0.9	12	12.5	66
French/Vienna	1 slice	1.0	13	12.6	70
honey wheatberry	1 slice	1.0	13	13.0	70
Italian	1 slice	0.6	7	14.9	78
mixed grain	1 slice	0.9	13	11.7	64
multigrain, "lite"	1 slice	0.5	10	9.6	45
pita, plain	1 large	0.8	3	46.8	240
pita, whole wheat	1 large	1.2	4	44.8	236
raisin	1 slice	1.0	13	13.2	70
Roman meal	1 slice	1.0	13	13.0	70
rye, American	1 slice	0.9	12	12.0	66
rye, pumpernickel	1 slice	0.8	9	15.4	82
sourdough	1 slice	1.0	13	12.0	70
wheat, commercial	1 slice	1.0	13	12.0	70
wheat, "lite"	1 slice	0.5	10	9.5	44
white, commercial	1 slice	1.0	13	13.0	70

*Although alcohol contains no fat, scientific evidence suggests that it may facilitate fat storage and hamper your weight-loss efforts. Excessive alcohol intake is detrimental to your health. We concur with other health organizations in recommending discretion in the use of alcoholic beverages.

	Serving	Total Fat g.	% Cal. from fat	Carbs. in g.	Cal.
white, hmde	1 slice	1.7	21	12.0	72
white, "lite"	1 slice	0.5	11	9.6	42
whole wheat, commercial	1 slice	1.0	13	12.0	70
bread crumbs	1 cup	4.6	11	73.4	392
breadsticks					
plain	1 small	0.3	7	7.5	39
sesame	1 small	2.2	39	6.3	51
bulgur, dry	1 cup	1.9	4	106.2	479
coffee cake	1 piece	6.9	27	37.7	232
cornbread					
from mix	⅛ mix	5.8	29	27.5	178
hmde	1 piece	7.3	33	28.7	198
cornmeal, dry	1 cup	2.2	4	107.0	585
cornstarch	1 T	0	0	7.3	31
crackers					
cheese	5 pieces	4.9	54	7.8	81
Cheese Nips	13 crackers	3.0	39	9.0	70
cheese w/peanut butter	2-oz. pkg.	12.0	39	36.0	280
Goldfish, any flavor	12 crackers	1.2	39	3.8	28
graham	2 squares	1.5	23	10.8	60
graham, crumbs	½ cup	4.0	15	44.0	240
Hi Ho	4 crackers	4.0	51	9.0	70
matzohs	1 board	1.9	15	22.0	115
melba toast	1 piece	0.1	6	6.9	15
Norwegian flatbread	2 thin	0.3	7	8.0	40
oyster	33 crackers	3.3	27	17.5	109
Premium Fat Free	5 crackers	0	0	12.0	50
rice cakes	1 piece	0.2	5	8.0	35
Ritz	3 crackers	3.0	9	6.7	53
Ritz cheese	3 crackers	2.5	56	3.5	40
rye w/cheese	1.5-oz. pkg.	9.5	42	22.0	205
Ryekrisp, plain	2 crackers	0.2	5	13.0	40
Ryekrisp, sesame	2 crackers	1.4	21	12.0	60
saltines	2 crackers	0.6	21	4.4	26
sesame wafers	3 crackers	3.0	39	9.5	70
Sociables	6 crackers	3.0	39	9.0	70
soda	5 crackers	1.9	27	10.0	63
toasted w/peanut butter	1.5-oz. pkg.	10.8	47	22.2	206
Triscuit	2 crackers	1.3	29	6.7	40
Uneeda	2 crackers	1.3	29	6.7	40
Vegetable Thins	7 crackers	4.0	51	8.0	70
Wasa crispbread	1 piece	1.0	20	9.0	45
Waverly Wafers	2 crackers	1.5	39	5.0	35
Wheat Thins	4 crackers	1.5	39	4.5	35
Wheat Thins, nutty	4 crackers	2.3	52	5.1	40
wheat w/cheese	1.5-oz. pkg.	10.9	46	22.8	212
Wheatsworth	5 crackers	3.0	39	9.0	70

	Serving	Total Fat g.	% Cal. from fat	Carbs. in g.	Cal.
zwieback	2 crackers	1.2	18	10.4	60
croissant	1 small	7.0	37	22.0	170
croutons, commercial	¼ cup	2.2	34	8.5	59
Danish pastry	1 medium	14.0	47	34.0	270
doughnut					
cake	1 2.2 oz.	13.7	49	29.7	254
yeast	1 2.2 oz.	9.9	41	35.2	219
English muffin					
plain	1	1.1	28	26.2	135
w/raisins	1	1.0	6	31.0	150
whole wheat	1	2.0	11	33.0	170
flour					
buckwheat	1 cup	2.5	7	70.6	326
rice	1 cup	0.9	2	91.0	398
rye, medium	1 cup	2.2	5	81.0	400
soy	1 cup	18.6	45	25.8	373
wheat, cake	1 cup	0.9	2	93.7	436
white, all purpose	1 cup	1.4	3	104.3	499
white, bread	1 cup	3.0	7	79.5	401
white, self-rising	1 cup	1.2	2	94.4	436
whole wheat	1 cup	2.4	5	85.2	400
French toast					
frzn variety	1 slice	4.4	24	26.5	166
hmde	1 slice	6.7	39	17.2	153
hushpuppy	1 medium	5.5	32	17.5	153
muffins					
all types, commercial	1 large (3 oz.)	10.3	38	27.2	242
banana nut	1 large (4 oz.)	15.8	38	52.2	371
blueberry, from mix	1 medium	4.3	31	19.5	126
bran, hmde	1 medium	5.1	41	16.7	112
corn	1 medium	4.2	29	20.0	130
pancakes					
blueberry, from mix	3 medium	15.0	42	41.0	320
buckwheat, from mix	3 medium	8.0	31	35.0	230
buttermilk, from mix	3 medium	8.0	33	30.0	220
hmde	3 medium	5.7	28	27.6	186
"lite," from mix	3 medium	2.5	12	37.1	190
whole wheat, from mix	3 medium	1.0	6	34.5	161
phyllo dough	2 oz.	0	0	39.0	165
pie crust, plain	⅛ pie	7.5	56	11.9	121
popover	1	3.7	37	10.3	90
rice bran	1 oz.	6.2	45	13.0	125
rolls					
brown & serve	1	2.0	23	13.0	80
crescent	1	5.6	50	11.1	100

	Serving	Total Fat g.	% Cal. from fat	Carbs. in g.	Cal.
croissant	1 small	6.0	45	13.0	120
French	1	0.4	3	28.3	137
hamburger	1	2.1	17	20.1	114
hard	1	1.0	9	19.0	100
hot dog	1	2.1	17	20.1	114
kaiser/hoagie	1 medium	2.0	9	37.0	190
parkerhouse	1	1.0	15	9.0	60
raisin	1 large	1.9	10	36.7	179
sandwich	1	2.1	17	20.1	114
sesame seed	1	1.0	15	11.0	60
sourdough	1	1.0	9	19.0	100
submarine	1 medium	2.0	5	72.0	360
wheat	1	0.8	10	14.6	72
white, commercial	1	2.0	23	14.0	80
white, hmde	1	2.0	20	13.0	89
whole wheat	1	0.8	10	14.6	72
yeast, sweet	1	6.8	40	21.4	154
soft pretzel	1 medium	0	0	37.0	170
stuffing					
bread, from mix	½ cup	12.8	55	19.7	208
cornbread, from mix	½ cup	8.5	44	21.5	175
Stove Top	½ cup	8.8	45	20.3	175
sweet roll, iced	1 medium	6.8	40	21.4	154
tortilla					
corn (unfried)	1 medium	1.1	15	12.8	67
flour	1 medium	2.0	21	15.0	85
turnover, fruit filled	1	7.8	41	23.4	173
waffle					
frzn, Eggo	1	5.0	38	16.0	120
frzn, other	1 medium	3.2	30	14.2	95
hmde	1 large	12.6	46	27.7	245

Candy

	Serving	Total Fat g.	% Cal. from fat	Carbs. in g.	Cal.
butterscotch	6 pieces	1.0	8	26.9	113
candied fruit					
apricot	1 oz.	0.1	1	24.2	94
cherry	1 oz.	0.1	1	24.6	96
citrus peel	1 oz.	0.1	1	22.9	90
figs	1 oz.	0.1	1	20.6	84
candy bar					
Almond Joy	1 oz.	8.0	50	16.0	143
Baby Ruth	1 oz.	6.0	42	18.0	130
Bit-o-Honey	1 oz.	3.6	27	21.2	121
Butterfinger	1 oz.	6.0	42	19.0	130
Chunky	1 oz.	8.6	50	15.8	150
Golden Almond, Hershey	1 oz.	9.9	56	14.0	159
Heath	1 oz.	8.9	56	16.0	142

	Serving	Total Fat g.	% Cal. from fat	Carbs. in g.	Cal.
Kit Kat	1.13 oz.	9.2	49	19.8	169
Krackle, Hershey	1 oz.	8.4	49	19.9	153
Mars	1.7 oz.	11.0	41	30.0	240
milk choc., Hershey	1 oz.	8.9	51	16.7	156
milk choc. w/almonds	1 oz.	10.1	60	14.5	151
Milky Way	1 oz.	5.0	35	20.0	130
Mounds	1 oz.	7.5	49	16.2	137
Mr. Goodbar	1 oz.	9.1	56	14.3	145
Nestle's Crunch	1.06 oz.	8.0	51	18.0	140
Snickers	1 oz.	6.5	43	16.5	135
Special Dark, Hershey	1.02 oz.	8.5	34	17.3	145
Three Musketeers	1 oz.	4.0	28	23.0	130
Twix	1 oz.	6.7	44	17.8	136
candy-coated almonds	1 oz.	2.0	15	23.0	120
caramels					
plain or choc. w/nuts	1 oz.	4.6	34	20.0	121
plain or choc. w/o nuts	1 oz.	3.0	25	20.0	110
choc. chips					
milk choc.	¼ cup	10.5	42	28.5	225
semisweet	¼ cup	13.0	53	31.0	220
choc.-covered cherries	1 oz.	2.0	16	21.0	110
choc.-covered cream center	1 oz.	3.7	28	22.3	120
choc.-covered mint patty	1 small	1.2	24	8.9	45
choc.-covered peanuts	1 oz.	9.0	51	14.0	160
choc.-covered raisins	1 oz.	5.0	35	20.0	130
choc. kisses	9 pieces	13.0	53	23.0	220
choc. stars	13 pieces	8.0	45	19.0	160
English toffee	1 oz.	2.0	16	23.0	110
fudge					
choc.	1 oz.	2.3	19	22.5	108
choc. w/nuts	1 oz.	4.6	34	20.6	121
Good & Plenty	1 oz.	0.1	1	25.9	106
gumdrops	10 small	0	0	34.6	135
Gummy Bears	1 oz.	0	0	22.0	100
hard candy	6 pieces	0	0	27.8	106
jelly beans	1 oz.	0	0	26.0	100
licorice	1 oz.	1.0	9	23.0	100
Life Savers	5 pieces	0	0	10.0	40
M&M's					
choc. only	1 oz.	6.0	39	20.0	140
peanut	1 oz.	7.0	42	17.0	150
malted-milk balls	1 oz.	5.0	35	21.0	130
marshmallow	1 large	0	0	6.0	25
mints	5 pieces	0	0	10.0	40
peanut brittle	1 oz.	5.4	38	19.7	128
Peanut Butter Cups, Reese's	0.6 oz.	6.0	54	9.0	100
Peppermint Pattie	1 oz.	3.9	23	33.6	149

	Serving	Total Fat g.	% Cal. from fat	Carbs. in g.	Cal.
praline	1 oz.	6.9	49	1.7	128
Reese's Pieces	1 oz.	6.0	39	17.0	140
sour balls	1 oz.	0	0	27.0	110
Starburst fruit chews	1 oz.	2.5	19	24.0	120
Sugar Daddy caramel	1.4 oz.	1.0	6	33.0	150
taffy	1 oz.	1.0	1	24.0	100
Tootsie Roll pop	1 oz.	0.6	5	26.4	111
Tootsie Roll	1 oz.	2.5	20	22.8	112
yogurt-covered peanuts	½ cup	25.0	50	47.0	450

Cereals

	Serving	Total Fat g.	% Cal. from fat	Carbs. in g.	Cal.
All Bran	⅓ cup	1.0	13	22.0	70
Alpha-Bits	1 cup	0.7	6	24.1	111
Apple Jacks	1 cup	0.1	1	25.7	110
bran, 100%	½ cup	1.4	17	20.7	76
bran, unprocessed, dry	¼ cup	0.6	17	9.7	32
Bran Buds	⅓ cup	1.0	13	22.0	70
Bran Chex	⅔ cup	1.0	1	25.0	100
Cap'n Crunch	¾ cup	2.0	15	24.0	120
Cheerios	1 cup	1.4	14	15.7	88
Cocoa Krispies	1 cup	0.5	3	33.6	147
Corn Chex	1 cup	0.2	2	25.0	110
cornflakes	1 cup	0.1	1	24.4	100
corn grits w/o added fat	½ cup	0.3	4	15.7	73
Cracklin' Oat Bran	⅓ cup	4.1	34	19.4	110
Cream of Wheat w/o added fat	½ cup	0.3	4	13.3	64
Crispix	1 cup	0	0	25.0	110
Fiber One	1 cup	2.0	15	46.0	120
Frosted Bran, Kellogg's	¾ cup	0	0	26.0	100
Frosted Mini-Wheats	4 biscuits	0.3	3	23.4	100
Fruit & Fibre					
w/apples & cinn.	⅔ cup	2.0	15	26.0	120
w/dates, raisins, walnuts	⅔ cup	2.0	15	27.0	120
Fruit Loops	1 cup	1.0	7	26.0	120
fruit squares, Kellogg's	¾ cup	0	0	44	180
Fruitful Bran	⅔ cup	0	0	29.0	110
Golden Grahams	¾ cup	1.1	9	24.1	110
granola					
commercial brands	⅓ cup	4.9	35	18.9	126
hmde	⅓ cup	10.0	49	20.8	184
low fat, Kellogg's	⅓ cup	2.0	15	25.0	120
Grapenut Flakes	1 cup	1.0	7	26.4	120
Grapenuts	¼ cup	0.1	1	23.1	105
Honeynut Cheerios	¾ cup	0.7	6	22.8	110
Kix	1½ cup	0.7	6	23.4	110
Life, plain or cinn.	1 cup	2.5	15	28.3	152
Mueslix, Kellogg's	⅔ cup	3.0	13	42.0	200

	Serving	Total Fat g.	% Cal. from fat	Carbs. in g.	Cal.
Nutri-Grain, Kellogg's					
almond raisin	⅔ cup	2.0	13	31.0	140
wheat	⅔ cup	0.3	3	24.0	100
oat bran, cooked cereal w/o added fat	½ cup	0.5	9	11.0	50
oat bran, dry	¼ cup	1.5	20	12.7	68
oats					
instant	1 packet	1.7	15	18.1	104
w/o added fat	½ cup	1.2	15	12.6	72
Product 19	1 cup	0.2	2	25	110
puffed rice	1 cup	0	0	12.6	56
puffed wheat	1 cup	0.1	2	9.6	44
Raisin Bran	1 cup	37.1	0.9	5	154
Rice Chex	1 cup	0.1	1	22.5	100
Rice Krispies	1 cup	0.2	2	24.8	112
shredded wheat	1 cup	0.3	3	18.8	83
Shredded Wheat Squares, fruit filled	½ cup	0	0	23.0	90
Special K	1 cup	0.1	1	21.3	111
Sugar Frosted Flakes	1 cup	0.5	3	34.0	148
Sugar Smacks	1 cup	0.7	4	33.0	141
Total	1 cup	1.0	9	24.0	100
Total raisin bran	1 cup	1.0	6	33.0	140
Wheat Chex	1 cup	1.2	6	37.8	169
wheat germ, toasted	¼ cup	2.8	24	14.9	104
Wheaties	1 cup	0.5	5	22.6	100
whole wheat, natural, w/o added fat	½ cup	0.5	6	16.6	75

Cheeses

	Serving	Total Fat g.	% Cal. from fat	Carbs. in g.	Cal.
American					
processed	1 oz.	8.9	75	0.5	106
reduced calorie	1 oz.	2.0	36	1.0	50
blue	1 oz.	8.2	74	0.7	100
Borden's Fat Free	1 oz.	< 0.5	12	3.0	38
Borden's Lite Line	1 oz.	2.0	36	1.0	50
Brie	1 oz.	7.9	75	0.1	95
caraway	1 oz.	8.3	70	0.9	107
cheddar					
grated	¼ cup	9.4	74	0.4	114
sliced	1 oz.	9.4	74	0.4	114
cheese spread (Kraft)	1 oz.	6.0	66	2.5	82
Cheez Whiz	1 oz.	5.7	67	1.8	77
Colby	1 oz.	9.1	73	0.7	112
cottage cheese					
1% fat	½ cup	1.2	13	3.1	82
2% fat	½ cup	2.2	20	4.1	101
creamed	½ cup	5.1	39	3.0	117
cream cheese					
Kraft Free	1 oz. (2 T)	0	0	2.0	30

	Serving	Total Fat g.	% Cal. from fat	Carbs. in g.	Cal.
"lite" (Neufchâtel)	1 oz. (2 T)	6.0	77	1.0	70
regular	1 oz. (2 T)	9.9	90	0.8	99
Edam	1 oz.	7.9	70	0.4	101
feta	1 oz.	6.0	72	1.2	75
Gouda	1 oz.	7.8	70	0.6	101
hot pepper cheese	1 oz.	8.9	76	0.5	106
Jarlsberg	1 oz.	7.0	63	1.0	100
Kraft American Singles	1 oz.	7.5	75	3.0	90
Kraft Free Singles	1 oz.	0	0	4.0	45
Kraft Light Singles	1 oz.	4.0	51	2.0	70
Limburger	1 oz.	7.7	75	0.1	93
Monterey Jack	1 oz.	8.6	73	0.2	106
mozzarella					
part skim	1 oz.	4.5	56	0.8	72
part skim, low moisture	1 oz.	4.9	56	0.9	79
whole milk	1 oz.	6.1	69	0.6	80
whole milk, low moisture	1 oz.	7.0	70	1.0	90
Muenster	1 oz.	8.5	74	0.3	104
Parmesan					
grated	1 T	1.5	59	0.2	23
hard	1 oz.	7.3	59	0.9	111
Weight Watchers Fat Free	1 T	0	0	2.0	15
pimento cheese spread	1 oz.	8.9	76	0.5	106
port wine, cold pack	1 oz.	8.0	72	0.2	100
provolone	1 oz.	7.6	68	0.6	100
ricotta					
"lite" reduced fat	½ cup	4.0	45	4.0	180
part skim	½ cup	9.8	52	6.4	171
whole milk	½ cup	16.1	67	3.8	216
Romano	1 oz.	7.6	62	1.0	110
Roquefort	1 oz.	8.7	75	0.6	105
Sargento Preferred Light					
mozzarella	1 oz.	3.0	45	0	60
Swiss	1 oz.	4.0	51	< 1.0	70
smoked cheese product	1 oz.	7.0	63	1.0	100
Swiss					
processed	1 oz.	7.1	67	0.6	95
sliced	1 oz.	7.8	66	1.0	107
Weight Watchers, slices	1 oz.	2.0	60	0	30

Combination Foods

	Serving	Total Fat g.	% Cal. from fat	Carbs. in g.	Cal.
baked beans w/pork	½ cup	2.0	14	25.2	133
beans & franks, canned	1 cup	16.8	42	39.4	364
beans					
refried, canned	½ cup	1.4	10	23.3	134

	Serving	Total Fat g.	% Cal. from fat	Carbs. in g.	Cal.
refried w/fat	½ cup	13.2	44	23.3	271
refried w/sausage, canned	½ cup	13.0	60	13.0	194
beef & vegetable stew	1 cup	10.5	43	15.2	218
beef burgundy	1 cup	19.8	53	13.1	337
beef pot pie					
frzn	8 oz.	31.0	65	27.0	430
hmde	8 oz.	30.5	53	39.5	517
beef short ribs w/gravy, frzn	5¾ oz.	20.0	52	12.0	350
beef stew, canned	1 cup	7.0	30	15.0	207
beef teriyaki, Stouffer's	10 oz.	8.0	25	37.0	290
burrito					
bean w/cheese	1 large	11.0	30	45.0	330
beef	1 large	19.0	41	47.3	413
cabbage roll w/beef & rice	1 medium	6.0	32	17.0	168
casserole, meat, veg., rice, sauce	1 cup	17.0	43	29.0	360
cheese soufflé	1 cup	16.2	70	5.9	207
chicken, glazed, Lean Cuisine	8½ oz.	7.0	25	24.0	250
Chicken à la king, hmde	1 cup	34.3	66	12.3	468
chicken à la king w/rice, frzn	1 cup	12.0	30	45.0	360
chicken & dumplings	1 cup	10.4	38	16.0	248
chicken & rice casserole	1 cup	17.0	43	29.0	360
chicken cacciatore, Stouffer's	11¼ oz.	11.0	32	29.0	310
chicken divan, Stouffer's	8 oz.	11.0	45	9.0	220
chicken fricassee, hmde	1 cup	22.3	52	7.4	386
chicken-fried steak	3½ oz.	23.4	59	15.9	355
chicken noodle casserole	1 cup	15.0	44	21.0	310
chicken parmigiana, hmde	7 oz.	14.8	43	22.7	308
chicken pot pie					
frzn	8 oz.	21.0	46	41.0	410
hmde	8 oz.	31.4	52	42.5	546
chicken salad, regular	½ cup	20.0	70	12.0	256
chicken tetrazzini	1 cup	19.6	49	28.0	360
chili					
w/beans	1 cup	14.0	44	30.4	286
w/o beans	1 cup	33.5	73	12.1	412
chop suey w/o rice					
beef	1 cup	17.0	51	13.0	300
fish or poultry	1 cup	4.0	26	7.0	141
chow mein					
beef, canned, La Choy	1 cup	1.0	13	9.0	70
chicken, canned, La Choy	1 cup	3.0	34	8.0	80
chicken, hmde	1 cup	10.0	35	10.0	255
pepper, La Choy	1 cup	2.0	23	10.0	80
corned-beef hash	1 cup	24.0	60	19.0	360
crab cake	1 small	3.8	56	0.2	61
creamed chipped beef	1 cup	25.2	60	17.4	377
deviled crab	½ cup	12.0	45	25.0	240

	Serving	Total Fat g.	% Cal. from fat	Carbs. in g.	Cal.
deviled egg	1 large	5.3	76	0	63
egg foo yung w/sauce	1 piece	3.5	39	9.5	80
egg salad	½ cup	23.0	78	4.0	267
eggplant Parmesan, traditional	1 cup	19.0	49	29.0	350
egg roll					
restaurant	1 (3½ oz.)	6.0	30	23.0	180
frzn, La Choy	4	4.0	30	16.0	120
enchilada					
bean, beef, & cheese	1 piece	13.0	43	28.0	270
beef, frzn	7½ oz.	16.0	44	37.0	324
cheese, frzn	8 oz.	18.9	53	28.5	320
chicken, frzn	7½ oz.	11.0	40	21.3	247
falafel	1 small	5.0	48	9.0	94
fettuccine Alfredo	1 cup	28.4	60	30.6	427
fillet of fish divan, frzn	12⅜ oz.	10.0	33	16.0	270
fritter, corn	1 medium	7.5	51	13.9	132
frzn dinner					
chopped beefsteak	11 oz.	21.0	50	24.0	376
chopped steak	18 oz.	46.0	56	52.0	740
fried chicken	11 oz.	28.0	46	56.0	560
meat loaf	19 oz.	38.0	61	49.0	560
turkey	11 oz.	11.0	29	43.0	340
green pepper stuffed w/rice & beef	1 average	11.0	44	18.0	225
ham salad w/mayo	½ cup	18.4	64	12.8	259
Hamburger Helper, all varieties	1 cup	15.7	41	30.0	341
lasagna					
cheese, frzn	10½ oz.	14.0	33	36.0	385
hmde w/beef & cheese	1 piece	17.0	38	38.0	400
zucchini lasagna, Lean Cuisine	11 oz.	7.0	24	28.0	260
lobster					
Newburg	½ cup	13.3	49	16.4	243
salad	½ cup	8.5	53	4.9	145
macaroni & cheese					
from package	1 cup	17.3	40	45.3	386
frzn	6 oz.	12.0	43	27.6	252
manicotti, cheese & tomato	1 piece	13.0	38	29.0	310
meatball (reg. ground beef)	1 medium	4.8	60	2.5	72
meat loaf, w/reg. ground beef	3½ oz.	20.4	55	10.8	332
onion rings	10 average	16.0	58	22.0	250
oysters Rockefeller, traditional	6–8 oysters	14.3	58	13.2	223
pepper steak	1 cup	11.0	30	36.0	330
pizza					
cheese	1 slice	9.5	46	16.5	185
cheese, French bread, frzn	5⅛ oz.	13.0	34	41.0	340
combination w/meat	1 slice	15.0	50	23.0	269
deep dish, cheese	1 slice	13.5	29	49.0	426
pepperoni, frzn	¼ pizza	21.3	52	29.2	368

	Serving	Total Fat g.	% Cal. from fat	Carbs. in g.	Cal.
pizza rolls, Jeno's	3 pieces	6.0	45	11.5	120
pork, sweet & sour, w/rice	1 cup	7.5	25	52.3	270
quiche					
Lorraine (bacon)	⅛ pie	41.0	68	31.0	540
plain or vegetable	1 slice	17.6	51	45.0	312
ravioli, canned	1 cup	4.6	19	34.0	220
Salisbury steak w/gravy	8 oz.	22.0	66	12.0	300
salmon patty, traditional	3½ oz.	12.4	47	16.1	239
sandwiches					
BBQ beef on bun	1	16.8	39	38.2	392
BBQ pork on bun	1	12.2	31	34.1	359
BLT w/mayo	1	17.0	44	26.0	347
bologna & cheese	1	22.5	56	28.0	363
chicken w/mayo & lettuce	1	14.4	43	23.0	303
club w/mayo	1	20.8	32	41.7	590
corned beef on rye	1	12.0	38	26.0	286
cream cheese & jelly	1	22.0	52	35.2	380
egg salad	1	14.0	45	28.0	281
grilled cheese	1	29.0	59	26.0	443
ham, cheese, & mayo	1	15.5	39	33.3	353
ham salad	1	13.6	38	36.0	322
peanut butter & jelly	1	16.0	39	44.0	368
Reuben	1	45.0	61	32.0	667
roast beef & gravy	1	22.3	47	34.7	429
roast beef & mayo	1	20.0	43	26.0	418
sloppy joe on bun	1	15.0	36	40.0	375
sub w/salami & cheese	1	41.0	44	88.0	833
tuna salad	1	21.0	48	29.0	396
turkey & mayo	1	18.4	41	27.6	402
turkey breast & mustard	1	5.2	16	27.6	285
turkey ham on rye	1	9.0	34	23.0	239
shrimp salad	½ cup	9.0	60	6.0	135
spaghetti					
w/meat sauce	1 cup	11.7	31	38.7	332
w/red clam sauce	1 cup	7.3	26	23.7	250
w/tomato sauce	1 cup	8.8	31	37.0	260
w/white clam sauce	1 cup	19.5	42	33.4	416
SpaghettiOs, Franco American	1 cup	1.6	9	32.7	166
spinach soufflé	1 cup	18.4	76	2.8	218
stroganoff, beef, Stouffer's	9¾ oz.	20.0	46	28.0	390
sushi w/fish & vegetables	5 oz.	1.0	6	17.0	141
taco, beef	1 medium	13.0	42	15.0	276
tamale w/sauce	1 piece	6.0	57	8.0	95
tortellini, meat or cheese	1 cup	8.0	19	55.0	370
tostada w/refried beans	1 medium	11.0	41	27.0	243
Tuna Helper	1 cup	14.0	42	29.4	301
tuna noodle casserole	1 cup	13.0	38	31.0	310

	Serving	Total Fat g.	% Cal. from fat	Carbs. in g.	Cal.
tuna salad					
oil pack, w/mayo	½ cup	16.3	65	7.7	226
water pack, w/mayo	½ cup	10.5	55	7.7	170
veal parmigiana					
hmde	1 cup	22.0	49	34.0	400
frzn	5 oz.	13.8	43	25.0	287
veal scallopini	1 cup	19.0	42	14.0	412
Welsh rarebit	1 cup	22.0	58	20.0	340

Desserts and Toppings

	Serving	Total Fat g.	% Cal. from fat	Carbs. in g.	Cal.
apple brown betty	½ cup	5.1	20	45.5	230
baklava	1 piece	16.0	49	35.0	295
brownie					
choc., "light," from mix	1/24 pkg.	2.0	18	21.0	100
choc., Little Debbie	2 small	13.0	43	30.0	270
choc., plain	1 small	5.0	43	15.0	105
choc., w/nuts & icing	1	3.5	39	12.7	81
cake					
angel food	1/12 cake	0.1	1	35.7	161
banana w/frosting	1/12 cake	18.0	39	60.0	410
butter w/frosting	1/12 cake	18.0	51	61.0	320
carrot w/frosting	1/12 cake	18.0	39	59.0	410
choc. w/frosting	1/12 cake	19.0	41	58.0	420
coconut w/frosting	1/12 cake	18.1	41	54.3	395
devil's food, "light," from mix	1/12 cake	4.0	23	33.0	160
German choc. w/frosting	1/12 cake	19.0	41	59.0	420
gingerbread	2½" slice	4.3	22	32.2	174
lemon chiffon	1/12 cake	5.0	23	36.0	200
lemon w/frosting	1/12 cake	18.0	39	60.0	420
marble w/frosting	1/12 cake	18.0	39	59.0	410
pound	1/12 cake	9.0	41	28.0	200
pound, Entenmann fat free	1-oz. slice	0	0	15.0	70
shortbread w/fruit	1 piece	8.9	23	61.2	344
spice w/frosting	1/12 cake	18.0	39	36.0	420
sponge	1 piece	3.1	15	35.7	188
streusel swirl	1/12 cake	11.0	38	37.7	260
white w/frosting	1/12 cake	11.0	28	60.1	350
yellow w/frosting	1/12 cake	11.0	28	60.0	350
yellow, "light," from mix	1/12 cake	3.0	16	35.0	170
cheesecake, traditional	⅛ pie	16.3	57	24.3	257
cobbler					
w/biscuit topping	½ cup	5.1	20	45.5	230
w/pie-crust topping	½ cup	10.0	36	39.0	250
cookie					
animal	15 cookies	3.6	19	31.2	168
anisette toast	1 slice	1.0	8	23.0	109
arrowroot	1	1.0	45	3.0	20

	Serving	Total Fat g.	% Cal. from fat	Carbs. in g.	Cal.
Bordeaux, Pepperidge Farm	1	1.5	39	5.5	35
Capri, Pepperidge Farm	1	5.0	56	10.0	80
Chantilly, Pepperidge Farm	1	2.0	23	14.0	80
choc.	1	2.5	41	7.8	55
choc. chip, hmde	1	2.7	53	6.4	46
choc. chip, Pepperidge Farm	1	2.5	23	6.0	100
choc. sandwich (Oreo type)	1	2.0	36	8.0	50
Entenmann's fat free	2	0	0	17.0	80
fat-free Newtons	1	0	0	16.0	70
fig bar	1	1.0	17	10.6	53
Fig Newtons	1	1.0	15	11.0	60
gingersnap	1	1.6	42	4.7	34
graham cracker, choc. covered	1	2.0	40	5.5	45
Health Valley fat free	1	0	0	17.0	80
Lido, Pepperidge Farm	3	5.0	50	10.0	90
macaroon, coconut	1	3.4	51	6.6	60
Milano, Pepperidge Farm	1	3.0	45	7.5	60
molasses	1	3.0	34	13.0	80
oatmeal	1	3.1	34	12.4	83
oatmeal raisin	1	3.0	42	9.0	65
oatmeal, Pepperidge Farm, Wholesome Choice	1	1.0	15	11.0	60
peanut butter ·	1	4.4	47	9.9	84
Rice Krispie bar	1	0.9	23	6.5	36
shortbread	1	2.3	49	4.9	42
Snack Well's					
bite-size chocolate chip	6	1.0	15	11.0	60
cinnamon graham snacks	9	0	0	12.0	50
creme sandwich cookies	1	1.0	18	10.0	50
devil's food cookie cakes	1	0	0	13.0	60
oatmeal raisin	1	1.0	15	10.0	60
Social Tea biscuit	1	1.0	45	4.0	20
sugar	1	3.1	34	13.0	83
sugar wafers	2 small	3.7	36	13.9	92
vanilla-creme sandwich	1	2.0	36	7.0	50
vanilla wafers	3	2.0	30	11.0	60
cream puff w/custard	1	18.1	54	26.7	303
Creamsicle	1 bar	3.0	34	14.0	80
cupcake					
choc. w/icing	1	6.0	31	28.4	172
yellow w/icing	1	5.0	28	27.0	160
custard, baked	½ cup	6.6	40	15.1	148
date bar	1 bar	2.0	20	6.0	90
eclair w/choc. icing & custard	1 small	13.6	51	23.2	239
frosting/icing					
choc.	2 T	7.0	39	24.0	160
"light" varieties, ready-to-spread	1/12 tub	1.0	7	30.0	130

	Serving	Total Fat g.	% Cal. from fat	Carbs. in g.	Cal.
ready-to-spread	1/12 tub	7.0	39	24.0	160
vanilla or lemon	2 T	6.0	32	28.0	170
fruit ice, Italian	½ cup	0	0	29.0	120
fruitcake	1 piece	6.6	36	25.7	163
Fudgesicle	1 bar	1.0	9	20.0	100
gelatin					
low-cal.	½ cup	0	0	0.1	8
regular, sweetened	½ cup	0	0	18.9	80
granola bar	1 bar	5.7	39	17.0	131
Hostess					
cupcake	1	5.0	26	28.0	170
cupcake lights	1	1.5	11	26.0	120
Ding Dong	1	9.0	51	21.0	160
fruit snack pie	1	14.4	49	33.1	266
Ho Ho	1	6.0	45	17.0	120
honey bun	1	23.0	51	48.0	410
Snoball	1	7.0	39	24.0	160
Twinkie	1	4.0	26	25.0	140
Twinkie lights	1	1.5	11	24.0	120
Ice cream					
choc. (10% fat)	½ cup	8.0	48	15.0	150
choc. (16% fat)	½ cup	17.0	57	24.0	270
dietetic, sugar-free	½ cup	3.5	35	12.0	90
French vanilla soft serve	½ cup	11.3	54	19.1	189
Simple Pleasures (simpless)	½ cup	0.5	4	22.0	120
strawberry (10% fat)	½ cup	6.0	42	18.0	130
vanilla (10% fat)	½ cup	7.2	48	15.9	134
vanilla (16% fat)	½ cup	11.8	61	16.0	175
Weight Watchers	½ cup	0	0	19.0	80
ice cream bar					
choc. coated	1 bar	11.5	52	16.8	198
toffee krunch	1 bar	13.0	69	16.0	170
ice cream cone (cone only)	1 medium	0.3	6	9.3	45
ice cream sandwich	1	8.3	37	30.1	204
ice milk					
choc.	½ cup	2.0	18	18.0	100
soft serve, all flavors	½ cup	2.3	19	19.2	112
strawberry	½ cup	2.5	23	17.5	100
vanilla	½ cup	2.8	27	14.5	92
ladyfinger	1	2.0	30	8.0	60
Little Debbie					
devil square	1 square	5.5	37	20.5	135
Dutch apple bar	2 oz.	5.0	32	24.0	140
fudge krispie	2 oz.	7.0	24	48.0	260
oatmeal cremes	2 pieces	12.3	33	52.5	340
peanut-butter bar	2 bars	18.0	44	41.0	370
mousse, choc., hmde	½ cup	32.9	66	33.2	447

	Serving	Total Fat g.	% Cal. from fat	Carbs. in g.	Cal.
pie					
apple	⅛ pie	11.9	38	43.0	282
banana cream or custard	⅛ pie	10.6	38	35.0	252
blueberry	⅛ pie	12.7	40	41.2	286
Boston cream pie	⅛ pie	10.0	39	34.0	230
cherry	⅛ pie	13.3	39	45.3	308
choc. cream	⅛ pie	17.3	52	33.6	301
coconut cream or custard	⅛ pie	14.3	48	28.4	268
key lime	⅛ pie	19.0	44	50.3	388
lemon chiffon	⅛ pie	10.2	36	35.5	254
lemon meringue, traditional	⅛ pie	13.1	34	55.1	350
mincemeat	⅛ pie	13.6	38	48.6	320
peach	⅛ pie	12.6	38	45.1	301
pecan	⅛ pie	23.6	50	52.8	431
pumpkin	⅛ pie	12.8	48	27.9	241
raisin	⅛ pie	12.6	35	50.7	319
rhubarb	⅛ pie	12.6	38	45.1	299
strawberry	⅛ pie	7.3	36	28.7	184
sweet potato	⅛ pie	12.9	48	27.0	243
pie tart, fruit filled	1	19.0	41	60.0	420
Popsicle	1 bar	0	0	20.0	80
pudding					
any flavor except choc.	½ cup	4.3	23	28.4	165
bread	½ cup	7.4	31	30.9	212
choc. w/whole milk	½ cup	5.6	23	40.4	221
choc., D-Zerta	½ cup	0.4	5	11.3	65
from mix w/skim milk	½ cup	0	0	22.9	124
rice	½ cup	4.1	21	30.0	175
tapioca	½ cup	4.1	23	27.6	161
pudding pop, frzn	1 bar	2.0	23	13.0	80.0
sherbet	½ cup	1.0	7	28.0	130
Tasty Kake					
butterscotch Krimpet	1	2.6	23	19.0	103
choc. junior	1	12.3	32	57.1	341
coconut cream	1	20.2	48	46.0	377
fruit pie	1	11.4	30	57.4	342
jelly Krimpet	1	1.0	11	18.2	85
light creme-filled cupcakes	1	1.4	13	21.5	100
toppings					
butterscotch/caramel	3 T	0.1	<1.0	27.0	155
choc. fudge	2 T	4.0	33	18.0	110
choc. syrup, Hershey	2 T	0.4	5	16.4	73
marshmallow creme	3 T	0	0	34.5	135
milk choc. fudge	2 T	1.0	6	31.0	140
pecans in syrup	3 T	1.5	7	42.0	195
pineapple	3 T	0.2	1	36.0	150
strawberry	3 T	0	0	42.0	150

	Serving	Total Fat g.	% Cal from fat	Carbs. in g.	Cal.
whipped topping					
aerosol	¼ cup	3.6	74	2.4	44
from mix	¼ cup	2.0	45	4.0	40
frzn, tub	¼ cup	4.8	72	4.3	60
"lite"	1 T	<1.0	100	1.0	8
whipping cream					
heavy, fluid	1 T	5.6	97	0.4	52
light, fluid	1 T	4.6	94	0.4	44
turnover, fruit filled	1	7.9	47	23.2	173
yogurt, frzn					
low fat	½ cup	1.0	7	23.0	120
nonfat	½ cup	0	0	23.0	100

Eggs

	Serving	Total Fat g.	% Cal from fat	Carbs. in g.	Cal.
boiled-poached	1	5.0	61	0.6	74
fried w/½ t fat	1 large	7.0	70	0.6	91
omelet					
2 oz. cheese, 3 egg	1	41.0	71	2.6	516
plain, 3 egg	1	22.2	69	1.8	289
Spanish, 2 egg	1	17.2	61	7.2	254
scrambled w/milk	1 large	7.5	67	1.3	101
substitute, frzn	¼ cup	0	0	1.0	25
white	1 large	0	0	0.3	17
yolk	1 large	5.1	78	0.3	59

Fast Foods/Restaurants

(all listings are for standard servings for the given establishment unless otherwise noted)

	Serving	Total Fat g.	% Cal from fat	Carbs. in g.	Cal.
Arby's					
baked potato deluxe	1	36.4	52	59.0	621
beef 'n' cheddar sandwich	1	26.8	53	27.7	455
chicken breast sandwich	1	25.0	46	47.9	493
curly fries	1 order	17.7	47	43.0	337
french fries	1 order	13.2	48	29.8	246
ham & cheese sandwich	1	13.7	42	19.2	292
jamocha shake	1	10.5	26	59.1	368
junior roast-beef sandwich	1	10.8	45	21.0	218
light roast-beef deluxe	1	10.0	30	33.0	296
light roast-chicken deluxe	1	5.0	18	33.0	253
light roast-turkey deluxe	1	4.0	14	33.0	249
potato cakes	1 order	12.0	53	19.8	204
roast-beef sandwich	1 regular	14.8	38	31.6	353
roast-chicken club	1	33.0	49	40.0	610
roast-chicken salad	1	7.2	38	12.0	172
sausage biscuit	1	31.9	62	35.0	460
super roast-beef sandwich	1	22.1	40	50.4	501
Burger King					
apple pie	1	14.0	41	44.0	311

	Serving	Total Fat g.	% Cal. from fat	Carbs. in g.	Cal.
bacon double cheeseburger	1	31.0	54	26.0	515
bacon double cheeseburger deluxe	1	39.0	59	28.0	592
BK Broiler chicken sandwich, w/o sauce	1	8.0	27	28.0	267
cheeseburger	1	15.0	42	28.0	318
cheeseburger, deluxe	1	23.0	53	29.0	390
cheeseburger, double	1	27.0	50	29.0	483
chef salad	1	9.0	45	7.0	178
chicken sandwich	1	40.0	53	56.0	685
Chicken Tenders	1 order	13.0	49	14.0	236
chunky chicken salad	1	4.0	25	8.0	142
Croissan'wich w/bacon, egg, & cheese	1	24.0	60	19.0	361
Croissan'wich w/ham, egg, & cheese	1	21.0	55	19.0	346
Croissan'wich w/sausage, egg, & cheese	1	40.0	67	22.0	534
french fries, medium	1 order	20.0	53	36.0	341
French toast sticks	1 order	32.0	53	53.0	538
garden salad w/o dressing	1	5.0	47	8.0	95
hamburger	1	11.0	36	28.0	272
hamburger, deluxe	1	19.0	50	28.0	344
mini muffins, blueberry	1 order	14.0	43	37.0	292
Ocean Catch fish fillet	1	25.0	45	49.0	495
onion rings, regular	1 order	17.0	51	28.0	302
shakes					
choc.	1	10.0	28	49.0	326
strawberry	1	10.0	23	66.0	394
vanilla	1	10.0	27	51.0	334
side salad					
w/diet dressing	1	0	0	8.0	42
w/regular dressing	1	22.0	63	28.0	315
Whopper	1	36.0	53	45.0	614
Whopper w/cheese	1	44.0	56	47.0	706
Whopper, double beef	1	53.0	57	45.0	844
Whopper, double beef w/cheese	1	61.0	59	47.0	935
Dairy Queen					
banana split	1	11.0	19	93.0	510
Blizzard, strawberry	1 regular	16.0	19	92.0	740
breaded chicken fillet sandwich	1	20.0	42	37.0	430
breaded chicken fillet sandwich w/cheese	1	25.0	47	38.0	480
Breeze, strawberry	1 regular	1.0	1	90.0	590
Buster bar	1	29.0	58	40.0	450
cheese dog	1	21.0	57	24.0	330
cheeseburger	1	18.0	44	30.0	365
cheeseburger, double	1	34.0	54	31.0	570
chili dog	1	19.0	52	26.0	330

	Serving	Total Fat g.	% Cal. from fat	Carbs. in g.	Cal.
choc. sundae, regular	1	7.0	21	54.0	300
Dilly bar	1	13.0	56	21.0	210
DQ Homestyle Ultimate burger	1	47.0	60	30.0	700
DQ Sandwich, frozen treat	1	4.0	26	24.0	140
fish fillet sandwich	1	16.0	39	39.0	370
fish fillet sandwich w/cheese	1	21.0	45	40.0	420
french fries					
large	1 order	18.0	41	52.0	390
regular	1 order	14.0	42	40.0	300
small	1 order	10.0	43	29.0	210
garden salad, plain	1	13.0	59	7.0	200
grilled chicken fillet sandwich	1	8.0	24	33.0	300
hamburger	1	13.0	38	29.0	310
hamburger, double	1	25.0	49	29.0	460
hot dog	1	16.0	51	23.0	280
hot fudge brownie delight	1	29.0	37	102.0	710
ice cream cone, regular					
choc.	1	7.0	27	36.0	230
choc. dipped	1	16.0	44	40.0	330
vanilla	1	7.0	27	36.0	230
yogurt	1	< 1.0	5	38.0	180
onion rings	1 order	12.0	45	29.0	240
Peanut Buster parfait	1	32.0	41	94.0	710
shake, regular					
choc.	1	14.0	23	94.0	540
vanilla	1	14.0	24	88.0	520
yogurt strawberry sundae	1 regular	< 1.0	4	43.0	200
Dominos					
cheese pizza 12"	2 slices	10.1	24	56.3	376
deluxe pizza 12"	2 slices	20.4	37	59.2	498
pepperoni pizza 12"	2 slices	17.5	34	55.6	460
sausage/mushroom pizza 12"	2 slices	15.8	33	55.3	430
vegi feast pizza 12"	2 slices	10.2	18	18.5	498
Godfather's Pizza					
cheese pizza, large	1/10 pizza	9.0	27	39.0	297
combo pizza, large	1/10 pizza	19.0	39	42.0	437
Hardee's					
apple turnover	1	12.0	40	38.0	270
bacon biscuit	1	21.0	52	34.0	360
bacon cheeseburger	1	39.0	57	31.0	610
bagel, plain	1	3.0	13	37.0	200
Big Cookie Treat	1	13.0	47	31.0	250
Big Country Breakfast					
w/bacon	1	40.0	55	51.0	660
w/ham	1	33.0	48	51.0	620
w/sausage	1	57.0	60	51.0	850
Big Deluxe burger	1	30.0	54	32.0	500

	Serving	Total Fat g.	% Cal. from fat	Carbs. in g.	Cal.
biscuit 'n' gravy	1	24.0	50	45.0	440
blueberry muffin	1	19.0	43	51.0	400
cheeseburger	1	14.0	39	33.0	320
cheeseburger, ¼ lb.	1	29.0	52	34.0	500
chef salad	1	15.0	56	5.0	240
chicken fillet	1	13.0	32	44.0	370
chicken stix	6 pieces	9.0	39	13.0	210
fisherman's fillet	1	24.0	43	49.0	500
french fries, regular	1 order	11.0	43	30.0	230
fried chicken breast	1	24.0	52	17.0	412
garden salad	1	14.0	60	3.0	210
grilled chicken breast sandwich	1	9.0	26	34.0	310
grilled chicken salad	1	15.0	48	4.0	280
hamburger	1	10.0	33	33.0	270
Hash Rounds	1 order	14.0	55	24.0	230
hot dog	1	17.0	51	25.0	300
mushroom 'n' Swiss burger	1	27.0	50	33.0	490
pancakes	1 order	2.0	6	56.0	280
rise 'n' shine biscuit	1	18.0	51	34.0	320
roast-beef sandwich	1	11.0	33	32.0	300
sausage biscuit	1	28.0	57	34.0	440
side salad	1	0.9	40	1.0	20
steak biscuit	1	29.0	52	46.0	500
turkey club sandwich	1	16.0	37	32.0	390
Jack in the Box					
Breakfast Jack sandwich	1	13.0	38	30.0	307
cheeseburger	1	14.0	40	33.0	315
cheeseburger, Jumbo Jack	1	40.0	53	46.0	677
cheeseburger, Ultimate	1	69.0	66	33.0	942
chef salad	1	18.0	50	10.0	325
chicken fajita pita	1	8.0	25	29.0	292
chicken strips	4 pieces	14.0	36	28.0	349
chicken supreme sandwich	1	36.0	56	34.0	525
fish supreme sandwich	1	32.0	52	47.0	554
french fries, regular	1 order	19.0	48	43.0	353
grilled chicken fillet sandwich	1	17.0	37	33.0	408
grilled sourdough burger	1	50.0	63	34.0	712
hamburger	1	11.0	37	28.0	267
hamburger, Jumbo Jack	1	34.0	52	42.0	584
onion rings	1 order	23.0	54	39.0	382
pancake platter	1	22.0	32	87.0	612
scrambled egg platter	1	40.0	54	52.0	662
shake					
choc.	1	7.0	19	55.0	330
vanilla	1	6.0	17	57.0	320
supreme crescent	1	40.0	66	27.0	547
taco salad	1	31.0	55	28.0	503

	Serving	Total Fat g.	% Cal. from fat	Carbs. in g.	Cal.
Kentucky Fried Chicken (KFC)					
breast, extra crispy	1	22.3	58	14.0	344
breast, original recipe	1	16.5	56	10.8	267
Chicken Little sandwich	1	10.1	54	13.8	169
chicken nuggets	6 nuggets	17.4	57	13.2	276
coleslaw	1 order	6.6	50	13.2	119
Colonel's chicken sandwich	1	27.3	51	38.6	482
corn on the cob	1 ear	3.1	16	31.9	176
drumstick, extra crispy	1	14.0	61	6.1	205
drumstick, original recipe	1	8.5	52	4.2	146
french fries	1 order	12.0	44	31.1	244
Hot Wings	6	24.1	58	17.3	376
mashed potatoes & gravy	1 order	1.6	20	11.7	71
Rotisserie Gold Chicken					
Dark Quarter (skin removed)	1	12.2	51	0	217
White Quarter (as served)	1	18.7	50	0	335
White Quarter (skin removed)	1	5.9	27	0	199
thigh, extra crispy	1	29.8	66	14.4	406
thigh, original recipe	1	19.7	60	11.1	294
wing, extra crispy	1	18.6	66	9.3	254
wing, original recipe	1	11.7	59	6.0	178
Long John Silver's					
baked chicken dinner	1	17.0	24	85.0	630
batter-dipped fish	1 piece	12.0	51	13.0	210
batter-dipped shrimp	1 piece	4.0	60	4.0	60
Chicken Plank	1 piece	6.0	41	10.0	130
Chicken Planks (dinner)	3 pieces	37.0	39	96.0	860
chicken sandwich, baked	1	8.0	23	29.0	320
coleslaw	½ cup	6.0	39	20.0	140
corn cobbette	1	8.0	51	18.0	140
fish & fries	2-piece	35.0	44	72.0	720
Fish & More dinner	2-piece	42.0	44	92.0	860
fish sandwich (w/o sauce)	1	16.0	38	40.0	380
fish w/lemon crumb	1 dinner	14.0	20	89.0	640
french fries	1 order	6.0	32	26.0	170
hush puppies	3	6.0	26	30.0	210
Light Portion fish	1 dinner	4.0	11	49.0	320
Ocean chef salad, side	1	5.0	3	13.0	150
seafood chowder	7 oz.	6.0	39	10.0	140
seafood gumbo	7 oz.	8.0	60	4.0	120
seafood salad dinner	1	19.0	43	35.0	395
shrimp dinner	1	51.0	47	102.0	970
McDonald's					
apple bran muffin	1	0	0	46.0	190
bacon bits	1 pkg.	1.2	67	0.1	16
Big Mac	1	32.4	52	42.5	560
biscuit w/bacon, egg, & cheese	1	26.4	54	33.3	440

	Serving	Total Fat g.	% Cal. from fat	Carbs. in g.	Cal.
biscuit w/sausage	1	29.0	59	31.9	440
biscuit w/sausage & egg	1	34.5	60	32.6	520
biscuit w/spread	1	12.7	44	31.9	260
cheeseburger	1	13.8	40	31.2	310
chef salad w/o dressing	1	13.3	52	7.5	230
Chicken McNuggets	6 pieces	16.3	51	16.5	290
chunky chicken salad w/o dressing	1	3.4	22	5.3	140
cookies					
choc. chip	1 box	15.6	43	41.9	330
McDonaldland	1 box	9.2	29	47.1	290
croutons	1 pkg.	2.2	40	6.8	50
Danish, all varieties	1	18.0	39	53.2	420
Egg McMuffin	1	11.2	35	28.1	290
English muffin w/spread	1	4.6	24	26.7	170
Filet-O-Fish	1	26.1	53	37.9	440
french fries					
small	1 order	12.0	49	25.6	220
medium	1 order	17.1	48	36.3	320
large	1 order	21.6	49	45.9	400
frozen yogurt cone	1	0.8	7	22.0	100
garden salad w/o dressing	1	6.6	54	6.2	110
hamburger	1	9.5	33	30.6	260
hash browns	1 order	7.3	51	14.9	130
hotcakes w/margarine & syrup	1	9.2	20	74.4	410
McChicken sandwich	1	28.6	52	39.8	490
McLean Deluxe	1	10.0	28	35.0	320
McLean w/cheese	1	14.0	34	35.0	370
pie, apple	1	14.8	51	30.0	260
Quarter Pounder	1	20.7	45	34.0	410
Quarter Pounder w/cheese	1	29.2	50	35.1	520
sausage, pork	1	16.3	81	0	180
Sausage McMuffin	1	21.9	53	27.3	370
Sausage McMuffin w/egg	1	26.8	55	27.9	440
scrambled eggs (2)	1 order	9.8	63	1.2	140
shake					
choc.	1	1.7	5	66.0	320
strawberry	1	1.3	4	67.0	320
vanilla	1	1.3	4	60.0	290
sundae					
caramel	1	2.8	9	59.3	270
hot fudge	1	3.2	12	50.5	240
strawberry	1	1.1	5	49.2	210
Pizza Hut					
Hand-Tossed pizza					
cheese, medium	2 slices	18.0	33	57.0	492
pepperoni, medium	2 slices	22.0	37	62.0	540
supreme, medium	2 slices	30.0	46	53.0	589

	Serving	Total Fat g.	% Cal. from fat	Carbs. in g.	Cal.
Pan pizza					
cheese, medium	2 slices	20.0	35	55.0	518
pepperoni, medium	2 slices	23.0	41	50.0	500
supreme, medium	2 slices	26.0	43	50.0	540
Thin 'n' Crispy pizza					
cheese, medium	2 slices	17.0	38	37.0	398
pepperoni, medium	2 slices	20.0	43	36.0	413
supreme, medium	2 slices	22.0	43	41.0	459
Shoney's Restaurants					
All American burger	1	32.6	59	26.8	501
baked fish, light	1	1.4	7	2.4	170
baked potato (10 oz.)	1	0.3	1	61.1	264
charbroiled chicken	1	7.4	28	1.3	239
charbroiled chicken sandwich	1	17.0	34	28.1	451
charbroiled shrimp	1 order	3.0	19	3.0	138
chicken fillet sandwich	1	21.2	41	38.9	464
chicken tenders	1 order	20.4	47	16.6	388
country-fried steak	1	27.2	55	33.9	449
french fries (3 oz.)	1 order	7.5	43	28.9	189
garden salad, typical (9 oz. fresh veg./low-cal dress.)	1	1.8	11	22.6	150
Grecian bread	1	2.2	25	13.2	80
Hawaiian chicken	1	7.4	25	7.4	262
hot fudge sundae	1	22.0	44	60.0	451
lasagna	1	9.8	30	44.9	297
liver and onions	1	22.9	50	15.4	411
onion rings	each	3.1	54	5.0	52
pancakes	1	0.2	2	19.9	91
rice (3.5 oz.)	1	3.7	24	23.1	137
shrimper's feast	1	22.2	52	29.9	383
sirloin	6 oz.	24.5	62	0	357
spaghetti dinner	1	16.3	29	63.4	496
strawberry pie	1 slice	16.7	45	44.5	332
Taco Bell					
burrito, bean	1	14.0	28	63.0	447
burrito, beef	1	21.0	88	48.0	493
burrito, combo	1	16.0	35	46.0	407
burrito, Supreme	1	22.0	39	55.0	503
chilito	1	18.0	42	36.0	383
cinnamon twists	1 order	8.0	42	24.0	171
Mexican pizza	1	37.0	58	40.0	575
MexiMelt, beef	1	15.0	51	19.0	266
MexiMelt, chicken	1	15.0	53	19.0	257
nachos	1 order	18.0	47	37.0	346
nachos, Supreme	1 order	27.0	81	41.0	455
pintos 'n' cheese	1 order	9.0	43	19.0	190
soft taco	1	12.0	48	18.0	225

	Serving	Total Fat g.	% Cal. from fat	Carbs. in g.	Cal.
soft taco, chicken	1	10.0	77	18.0	210
soft taco, Supreme	1	16.0	63	19.0	272
taco	1	11.0	54	11.0	183
taco salad	1	61.0	55	55.0	905
tostada	1	11.0	41	27.0	243
Wendy's					
baked potato, plain	1	2.0	7	52.0	250
baked potato, w/cheese	1	21.0	40	57.0	470
Big Classic	1	33.0	52	46.0	570
breaded chicken sandwich	1	19.0	40	41.0	430
cheeseburger, single	1	20.0	45	28.0	400
cheeseburger, junior	1	13.0	38	34.0	310
chicken club sandwich	1	24.0	43	42.0	500
chili con carne	1 small	7.0	29	23.0	220
country fried steak sandwich	1	41.0	64	25.0	580
crispy chicken nuggets (6)	1	21.0	61	14.0	310
deluxe garden salad	1	5.0	44	9.0	102
fish fillet sandwich	1	25.0	49	42.0	460
french fries (small)	1 order	12.0	45	33.0	240
Frosty, choc., small	1	14.0	31	59.0	400
grilled chicken sandwich	1	9.0	25	37.0	320
hamburger, single	1	15.0	40	28.0	340
hamburger, double	1	33.0	52	46.0	570
hamburger, junior	1	9.0	31	30.0	260
taco salad	1	37.0	50	46.0	660

Fats

	Serving	Total Fat g.	% Cal. from fat	Carbs. in g.	Cal.
bacon fat	1 T	14.0	100	0	126
beef, separable fat	1 oz.	23.3	100	0	210
butter					
solid	1 t	4.0	100	0	36
solid	1 T	12.0	100	0	108
whipped	1 t	3.1	100	0	28
Butter Buds, liquid	2 T	0	0	4.0	12
butter sprinkles	½ t	0	0	<1.0	4
chicken fat, raw	1 T	12.8	100	0	115
cream					
light	1 T	2.9	90	0.6	29
medium (25% fat)	1 T	3.8	92	0.5	37
cream substitute					
liquid/frzn	½ fl. oz.	1.5	67	1.7	20
powdered	1 t	0.7	57	1.1	11
half & half	1 T	1.7	77	0.6	20
margarine					
liquid	1 t	4.0	100	0	36
reduced calorie, tub	1 t	2.0	100	0	18
solid (corn), stick	1 t	4.0	100	0	36

	Serving	Total Fat g.	% Cal. from fat	Carbs. in g.	Cal.
mayonnaise					
fat free	1 T	0	0	3.0	10
reduced calorie	1 T	5.0	90	1.0	50
regular (soybean)	1 T	11.0	100	0.4	100
no-stick spray (Pam, etc.)	2-sec. spray	0.9		0	8
oil					
canola	1 T	13.3	100	0	120
corn	1 T	13.3	100	0	120
olive	1 T	13.3	100	0	119
safflower	1 T	13.3	100	0	120
soybean	1 T	13.3	100	0	120
pork, separable fat, cooked	1 oz.	24.0	100	0	216
pork fat (lard)	1 T	12.8	100	0	116
salt pork, raw	1 oz.	23.8	98	0	219
sandwich spread (Miracle Whip type)	1 T	6.9	90	1.7	69
shortening, vegetable	1 T	12.0		0	108
sour cream					
cultured	1 T	2.5	86	0.5	26
fat free	1 T	0	0	3.0	10
half & half, cultured	1 T	1.8	81	0.6	20
imitation	1 T	2.7	81	1.0	30
"lite"	1 T	0.7	35	1.8	18

Fish

(all baked/broiled w/o added fat unless otherwise noted)

	Serving	Total Fat g.	% Cal. from fat	Carbs. in g.	Cal.
abalone, canned	3½ oz.	0.6	6	5.1	89
anchovy, canned	3 fillets	1.1	40	0	25
anchovy paste	1 t	0.8	51	0.5	14
bass					
freshwater	3½ oz.	4.7	29	0	145
saltwater, black	3½ oz.	1.2	12	0	93
saltwater, striped	3½ oz.	2.5	21	0	105
bluefish					
cooked	3½ oz.	5.36	31	0	157
fried	3½ oz.	12.8	56	6.5	205
butterfish					
northern	3½ oz.	10.2	50	0	184
northern, fried	3½ oz.	19.1	63	7.7	275
carp	3½ oz.	6.1	40	0	138
catfish	3½ oz.	3.1	27	0	103
catfish, breaded & fried	3½ oz.	13.2	53	6.8	226
caviar, black or red, granular	1 round t	1.0	69	0.2	13
clams					
canned, solids & liquid	½ cup	0.7	7	3.0	85
canned, solids only	3 oz.	1.6	12	4.1	118
meat only	5 large	1.0	13	2.5	67
soft, raw	4 large	0.8	11	2.2	63

	Serving	Total Fat g.	% Cal. from fat	Carbs. in g.	Cal.
cod					
canned	3½ oz.	0.8	7	0	104
cooked	3½ oz.	0.8	7	0	104
dried, salted	3½ oz.	2.3	7	0	287
crab					
canned	½ cup	0.9	12	0	67
deviled	3½ oz.	10.1	42	22.6	217
fried	3½ oz.	18.0	59	9.75	273
crab, Alaska king	3½ oz.	1.5	14	0	96
crab cake	3½ oz.	8.5	43	0.5	176
crayfish, freshwater	3½ oz.	1.4	11	0	113
dolphinfish	3½ oz.	0.8	8	0	93
eel, American					
cooked	3½ oz.	18.3	63	0	260
smoked	3½ oz.	23.6	75	0	281
eulachon (smelt)	3½ oz.	6.2	47	0	118
fillets, frzn					
batter dipped	2 pieces	25.8	52	37.6	447
light & crispy	2 pieces	15.9	48	27.3	301
fish cakes, frzn, fried	3½ oz.	8.8	44	22.7	181
flatfish	3½ oz.	0.8	9	0	79
flounder/sole	3½ oz.	0.5	7	0	68
gefilte fish	3½ oz.	1.7	18	7.4	84
grouper	3½ oz.	1.3	1	0	117
haddock					
cooked	3½ oz.	0.6	7	0	79
fried	3½ oz.	14.2	45	25.6	284
smoked/canned	3½ oz.	0.4	3	0	103
halibut	3½ oz.	1.2	11	0	100
herring					
canned or smoked	3½ oz.	10.0	52	19.6	174
cooked	3½ oz.	11.3	58	0	176
pickled	3½ oz.	17.9	62	9.6	260
Jack mackerel	3½ oz.	5.6	35	0	143
kingfish	3½ oz.	3.0	26	0	105
lobster, northern					
broiled w/fat	12 oz.	15.1	31	4.5	445
cooked	3½ oz.	0.6	5	1.33	97
mackerel					
Atlantic	3½ oz.	12.2	57	0	191
Pacific	3½ oz.	7.3	41	0	159
mussels					
canned	3½ oz.	4.5	25	7.4	163
meat only	3½ oz.	2.1	23	3.5	84
ocean perch					
cooked	3½ oz.	1.2	12	0	88
fried	3½ oz.	14.0	45	21.0	280

	Serving	Total Fat g.	% Cal. from fat	Carbs. in g.	Cal.
octopus	3½ oz.	2.1	11	4.3	163
oysters					
canned	3½ oz.	2.5	33	3.6	68
fried	3½ oz.	12.5	58	11.6	195
raw	5–8 medium	2.1	33	3.3	58
perch, freshwater, yellow	3½ oz.	0.9	9	0	91
pike					
blue	3½ oz.	0.9	9	0	90
northern	3½ oz.	1.1	11	0	88
walleye	3½ oz.	1.2	12	0	93
pollock, Atlantic	3½ oz.	1.0	10	0	91
pompano	3½ oz.	9.5	52	0	166
red snapper	3½ oz.	1.9	18	0	93
rockfish, oven steamed	3½ oz.	2.5	21	0	107
roughy, orange	3½ oz.	7.0	51	0	124
salmon					
Atlantic	3½ oz.	6.3	40	0	141
broiled/baked	3½ oz.	7.4	37	0	182
chinook, canned	3½ oz.	14.0	60	0	210
pink, canned	3½ oz.	5.1	39	0	118
smoked	3½ oz.	9.3	47	0	176
sardines					
Atlantic, in soy oil	2 sardines	2.8	50	0	50
Pacific, in tomato sauce	2 sardines	9.2	61	1	136
scallops					
cooked	3½ oz.	0.7	7	2.5	88
frzn, fried	3½ oz.	10.9	45	10.1	214
steamed	3½ oz.	0.7	7	2.5	88
sea bass, white	3½ oz.	1.5	14	0	96
shrimp					
canned, dry pack	3½ oz.	1.6	14	0.9	102
canned, wet pack	½ cup	1.3	15	0.7	77
fried	3½ oz.	12.2	46	11.5	240
raw or boiled	3½ oz.	1.8	15	0.8	105
smelt, canned	4–5 medium	13.5	61	0	200
sole, fillet	3½ oz.	0.5	7	0	68
squid					
fried	3 oz.	6.4	39	6.6	149
raw	3 oz.	1.2	14	2.6	78
surimi	3½ oz.	0.9	8	6.8	98
swordfish	3½ oz.	5.2	30	0	154
trout					
brook	3½ oz.	2.1	19	0	101
rainbow	3½ oz.	11.4	53	0	195
tuna					
albacore, raw	3½ oz.	7.5	38	0	177
bluefin, raw	3½ oz.	4.1	25	0	145

	Serving	Total Fat g.	% Cal. from fat	Carbs. in g.	Cal.
canned, light in oil	3½ oz.	8.1	37	0	197
canned, light in water	3½ oz.	0.8	6	0	115
canned, white in oil	3½ oz.	8.0	39	0	185
canned, white in water	3½ oz.	2.4	16	0	135
yellowfin, raw	3½ oz.	3.0	20	0	133
white perch	3½ oz.	3.9	31	0	114
whiting	3½ oz.	1.7	13	0	114
yellowtail	3½ oz.	5.4	35	0	138

Fruit

	Serving	Total Fat g.	% Cal. from fat	Carbs. in g.	Cal.
apple					
dried	½ cup	0.1	1	28.3	105
whole w/peel	1 medium	0.5	5	21.1	81
applesauce, unsweetened	½ cup	0.1	2	13.8	53
apricots					
dried	10 halves	0.2	2	21.6	83
fresh	3 medium	0.4	7	11.8	51
avocado					
California	1 (6 oz.)	30.0	88	12.0	306
Florida	1 (11 oz.)	27.0	72	27.1	339
banana	1 medium	0.6	5	26.7	105
banana chips	½ cup	8.0	29	15.0	248
blackberries					
fresh	1 cup	0.6	7	18.4	74
frzn, unsweetened	1 cup	0.7	7	23.7	97
blueberries					
fresh	1 cup	0.6	7	20.5	82
frzn, unsweetened	1 cup	1.0	11	18.8	78
boysenberries, frzn, unsweetened	1 cup	0.4	5	16.1	66
breadfruit, fresh	¼ small	0.2	2	26.0	99
cantaloupe	1 cup	0.4	6	13.4	57
cherries					
maraschino	¼ cup	0.2	3	16.6	66
sour, canned in heavy syrup	½ cup	0.1	1	29.8	116
sweet	½ cup	0.7	13	11.3	49
cranberries, fresh	1 cup	0.2	4	12.1	46
cranberry sauce	½ cup	0.2	1	53.7	209
cranberry–orange relish	½ cup	0.1	< 1	63.8	246
dates, whole, dried	10 dates	0.4	1	61.0	228
figs					
canned	3 figs	0.1	1	19.5	75
dried, uncooked	10 figs	2.2	4	122.2	477
fresh	1 medium	0.2	5	9.6	37
fruit cocktail, canned w/juice	1 cup	0.3	2	29.4	112
grapefruit	½ medium	0.1	2	9.5	37
grapes, Thompson seedless	½ cup	0.1	1	25.2	94
guava, fresh	1 medium	0.5	1	10.7	45

	Serving	Total Fat g.	% Cal. from fat	Carbs. in g.	Cal.
honeydew melon, fresh	¼ small	0.1	2	11.8	46
kiwi, fresh	1 medium	0.3	6	11.3	46
kumquat, fresh	1 medium	0	0	3.1	12
lemon, fresh	1 medium	0.2	11	5.4	17
lime, fresh	1 medium	0.1	5	7.1	20
mandarin oranges, canned w/juice	½ cup	0	0	11.9	46
mango, fresh	1 medium	0.6	4	35.2	135
melon balls, frzn	1 cup	0.4	7	13.7	55
mixed fruit					
dried	½ cup	0.5	2	64.1	243
frzn, sweetened	1 cup	0.5	2	60.6	245
nectarine, fresh	1 medium	0.6	8	16.0	67
orange					
naval, fresh	1 medium	0.1	1	16.3	65
Valencia, fresh	1 medium	0.4	6	14.4	59
papaya, fresh	1 medium	0.4	3	29.8	117
passionfruit, purple, fresh	1 medium	0.1	5	4.2	18
peach					
canned in heavy syrup	1 cup	0.3	1	51.0	190
canned in light syrup	1 cup	0.1	1	36.5	136
canned, water pack	1 cup	0.1	1	14.9	58
fresh	1 medium	0.1	2	9.7	37
frzn, sweetened	1 cup	0.3	1	59.9	235
pear					
canned in heavy syrup	1 cup	0.3	1	48.9	188
canned in light syrup	1 cup	0.1	1	38.1	144
fresh	1 medium	0.7	6	25.1	98
persimmon, fresh	1 medium	0.1	3	8.4	32
pineapple pieces					
canned, unsweetened	1 cup	0.2	1	39.2	150
fresh	1 cup	0.7	8	19.2	77
plantain, cooked, sliced	1 cup	0.3	1	48.0	179
plum					
canned in heavy syrup	½ cup	0.1	1	30.9	119
fresh	1 medium	0.4	1	8.6	36
pomegranate, fresh	1 medium	0.5	4	26.4	104
prickly pear, fresh	1 medium	0.5	11	9.9	42
prunes, dried, cooked	½ cup	0.2	1	29.8	113
raisins					
dark seedless	¼ cup	0.2	2	29.7	112
golden seedless	¼ cup	0.2	2	29.8	113
raspberries					
fresh	1 cup	0.7	10	14.2	61
frzn, sweetened	1 cup	0.4	1	65.4	256
rhubarb, diced, unsweetened	1 cup	0.2	7	5.6	26
strawberries					
fresh	1 cup	0.6	12	10.5	45

	Serving	Total Fat g.	% Cal. from fat	Carbs. in g.	Cal.
frzn, sweetened	1 cup	0.3	1	66.1	245
frzn, unsweetened	1 cup	0.2	3	13.6	52
sugar apples, fresh	1 medium	0.5	3	36.6	146
tangelo, fresh	1 medium	0.1	2	9.5	39
tangerine, fresh	1 medium	0.2	5	9.4	37
watermelon, fresh	1 cup	0.5	9	11.5	50

Fruit Juices & Nectars

	Serving	Total Fat g.	% Cal. from fat	Carbs. in g.	Cal.
apple juice	1 cup	0.3	2	29.0	116
carrot juice	1 cup	0.4	4	22.8	97
cranberry juice cocktail					
low cal	1 cup	0	0	11.2	45
regular	1 cup	0.1	1	34.4	144
cranberry–apple juice	1 cup	0.2	1	40.0	160
grape juice	1 cup	0.2	1	31.9	128
grapefruit juice	1 cup	0.2	2	22.1	93
lemon juice	1 T	0	0	1.3	5
lime juice	1 T	0	0	1.4	6
orange juice	1 cup	0.5	4	25.8	111
orange-grapefruit juice	1 cup	0.2	2	25.4	107
peach juice or nectar	1 cup	0.1	1	34.7	134
pear juice or nectar	1 cup	0	0	39.4	149
pineapple juice	1 cup	0.2	1	34.4	139
pineapple-orange juice	1 cup	0.1	1	30.6	133
prune juice	1 cup	0.1	0	44.7	181
tomato juice	1 cup	0.2	4	10.2	43
V8 juice	1 cup	0.1	2	10.2	49

Gravies, Sauces, and Dips

	Serving	Total Fat g.	% Cal. from fat	Carbs. in g.	Cal.
au jus, mix	½ cup	0.3	11	3.7	24
barbecue sauce	1 T	0.3	23	2.0	12
béarnaise sauce, mix	¼ pkg.	25.6	88	6.6	263
beef gravy, canned	½ can	2.8	41	5.6	62
brown gravy					
from mix	½ cup	0.9	21	6.5	38
hmde	¼ cup	14.0	77	8.5	164
chicken gravy					
canned	½ can	6.5	61	6.8	95
from mix	½ cup	0.9	20	7.1	41
giblet from can	¼ cup	1.5	47	2.7	29
chili sauce	1 T	0	0	3.8	17
dip made with sour cream	2 T	3.0	67	2.0	40
enchilada dip, Frito's	1 oz.	2.0	45	5.0	40
guacamole dip	1 oz.	4.0	72	3.0	50
hollandaise sauce	¼ cup	18.0	95	5.0	170
home-style gravy, from mix	¼ cup	0.1	6	3.1	16
ketchup, tomato	1 T	0.1	6	4.1	16

	Serving	Total Fat g.	% Cal. from fat	Carbs. in g.	Cal.
mushroom gravy					
canned	½ can	4.0	48	8.1	75
from mix	½ cup	0.4	10	6.9	35
mushroom sauce, from mix	¼ pkg.	3.2	41	7.4	71
mustard					
brown	1 T	0.9	54	0.9	15
yellow	1 T	0.6	45	0.9	12
onion dip	2 T	4.0	80	2.0	45
onion gravy, from mix	½ cup	0.4	9	8.1	39
pesto sauce, commercial	1 oz.	14.6	85	3.0	155
pork gravy, from mix	½ cup	0.9	21	6.7	38
sour-cream sauce	¼ cup	7.6	53	11.4	128
soy sauce	1 T	0	0	1.1	10
soy sauce, reduced sodium	1 T	0	0	1.5	11
spaghetti sauce					
"healthy"/"lite" varieties	½ cup	1.0	15	9.0	60
hmde, w/reg. ground beef	½ cup	18.7	69	11.5	243
meat flavor, jar	½ cup	6.0	39	20.0	140
meatless, jar	½ cup	2.0	25	12.0	70
mushroom, jar	½ cup	2.0	26	12.0	70
spinach dip (sour cream & mayo)	2 T	7.1	86	2.0	74
steak sauce					
A-1	1 T	0	0	3.0	12
others	1 T	0	0	4.0	17
stroganoff sauce, mix	¼ pkg.	2.9	36	9.1	73
sweet & sour sauce	¼ cup	0.2	2	24.0	100
tabasco sauce	1 t	0	0	0	1
taco sauce	1 T	0	0	1.3	5
tartar sauce	1 T	7.7	99	0.1	70
teriyaki sauce	1 T	0	0	2.9	15
turkey gravy					
canned	½ can	3.1	37	7.6	76
from mix	½ cup	0.9	19	7.5	43
white sauce	2 T	3.4	51	5.4	60
Worcestershire sauce	1 T	0	0	2.0	10

Meats

(all cooked w/o added fat unless otherwise noted)

beef, extra lean, ≤ 5% fat (cooked)

	Serving	Total Fat g.	% Cal. from fat	Carbs. in g.	Cal.
Healthy Choice lean ground beef	3½ oz.	3.5	28	0	114
round, eye of, lean	3½ oz.	3.5	20	0	155
beef, lean, 5–10% fat (cooked)					
arm/blade, lean pot roast	3½ oz.	9.4	41	0	207
flank steak, fat trimmed	3½ oz.	8.0	37	0	193
hindshank, lean	3½ oz.	9.4	41	0	207
porterhouse steak, lean	3½ oz.	10.4	42	0	225

	Serving	Total Fat g.	% Cal. from fat	Carbs. in g.	Cal.
rib steak, lean	3½ oz.	9.4	41	0	207
round					
bottom, lean	3½ oz.	9.4	41	0	207
roasted	3½ oz.	7.4	35	0	189
rump, lean, pot-roasted	3½ oz.	7.0	35	0	179
top, lean	3½ oz.	6.4	27	0	211
short plate, separable lean only	3½ oz.	10.4	42	0	225
sirloin steak, lean	3½ oz.	8.9	40	0	201
sirloin tip, lean, roasted	3½ oz.	9.4	41	0	207
tenderloin, lean, broiled	3½ oz.	11.1	46	0	219
top sirloin, lean, broiled	3½ oz.	7.9	35	0	201
beef, regular, 11–17.4% fat (cooked)					
chuck, separable lean	3½ oz.	15.2	51	0	268
club steak, lean	3½ oz.	12.9	48	0	240
cubed steak	3½ oz.	15.4	53	0	264
hamburger					
extra lean	3 oz.	13.9	49	0	253
lean	3 oz.	15.7	53	0	268
rib roast, lean	3½ oz.	15.2	52	0	264
sirloin tips, roasted	3½ oz.	15.2	52	0	264
stew meat, round, raw	4 oz.	15.3	47	0	294
T-bone, lean only	3½ oz.	10.3	44	0	212
tenderloin, marbled	3½ oz.	15.2	52	0	264
beef, high fat, ≥ 17.5% fat (cooked)					
arm/blade, pot-roasted	3½ oz.	26.5	67	0	354
chuck, ground	3½ oz.	23.9	66	0	327
hamburger, regular	3 oz.	19.6	62	0	286
meatballs	1 oz.	5.5	63	0	78
porterhouse steak, lean & marbled	3½ oz.	19.6	62	0	286
rib steak	3½ oz.	14.7	46	0	286
rump, pot-roasted	3½ oz.	19.6	62	0	286
short ribs, lean	3½ oz.	19.6	62	0	286
sirloin, broiled	3½ oz.	18.7	61	0	278
sirloin, ground	3½ oz.	26.5	67	0	354
T-bone, broiled	3½ oz.	26.5	67	0	354
beef, highest fat, ≥ 27.5% fat (cooked)					
brisket, lean & marbled	3½ oz.	30.0	73	0	367
chuck, stew meat	3½ oz.	30.0	73	0	367
corned, medium fat	3½ oz.	30.2	73	0	372
rib roast	3½ oz.	30.0	73	0	367
ribeye steak, marbled	3½ oz.	38.8	79	0	440
short ribs	3½ oz.	31.7	75	0	382
lamb					
blade chop					
lean	1 chop	6.4	45	0	128
lean & marbled	3½ oz.	26.1	62	0	380

	Serving	Total Fat g.	% Cal. from fat	Carbs. in g.	Cal.
leg					
lean	3½ oz.	8.1	41	0	180
lean & marbled	3½ oz.	14.5	54	0	242
loin chop					
lean	3½ oz.	8.1	41	0	180
lean & marbled	3½ oz.	22.5	67	0	302
rib chop					
lean	3½ oz.	8.1	41	0	180
lean & marbled	3½ oz.	21.2	65	0	292
shoulder					
lean	3½ oz.	9.9	36	0	248
lean & marbled	3½ oz.	27.0	57	0	430
miscellaneous meats					
bacon substitute (breakfast strip)	2 strips	4.8	86	1.0	50
beefalo	3½ oz.	6.3	30	0	188
frog legs					
cooked	4 large	0.3	3	0	73
flour-coated & fried	6 large	28.6	61	0	418
rabbit, stewed	3½ oz.	10.1	42	0	216
venison, roasted	3½ oz.	2.5	14	0	157
organ meats					
brains, all kinds, raw	3 oz.	7.4	63	0	106
heart					
beef, lean, braised	3½ oz.	5.6	29	0.4	175
calf, braised	3½ oz.	6.8	33	0.1	186
hog, braised	3½ oz.	6.5	31	0.5	191
kidney, beef, braised	3½ oz.	3.4	21	1.0	144
liver					
beef, braised	3½ oz.	4.9	27	3.4	161
beef, pan fried	3½ oz.	8.0	33	7.9	217
calf, braised	3½ oz.	6.9	38	2.7	165
calf, pan fried	3½ oz.	11.4	42	3.9	245
tongue					
beef, etc., pickled	1 oz.	4.6	66	1.0	63
beef, etc., potted	1 oz.	4.7	63	0.3	67
beef, med. fat, braised	3½ oz.	18.6	62	0	271
pork					
bacon					
cured, broiled	1 slice	3.1	78	0	36
cured, raw	1 slice	13.0	93	0	126
bacon bits	1 T	1.0	43	0.2	21
blade					
lean	3½ oz.	9.6	39	0	219
lean, marbled	3½ oz.	18.0	56	0	290
Boston butt					
lean	3½ oz.	14.2	42	0	304
lean & marbled	3½ oz.	26.8	74	0	327

	Serving	Total Fat g.	% Cal. from fat	Carbs. in g.	Cal.
Canadian bacon, broiled	1 oz.	1.8	36	2.0	45
ham					
cured, butt, lean	3½ oz.	5.5	34	1.5	145
cured, butt, lean & marbled	3½ oz.	12.9	57	0.1	203
cured, canned	3 oz.	4.6	35	0	120
cured, shank, lean	3½ oz.	6.3	35	1.2	164
cured, shank, lean & marbled	2 slices	13.8	49	0	255
fresh, lean	3½ oz.	6.4	26	0	222
fresh, lean, marbled & fat	3½ oz.	18.3	54	0	306
ham & cheese loaf	3½ oz.	20.0	70	1.4	256
smoked	3½ oz.	7.0	45	3.5	140
smoked, 95% lean	3½ oz.	3.5	30	3.5	105
loin chop					
lean	1 chop	7.7	41	0	170
lean & fat	1 chop	22.5	64	0	314
picnic					
cured, lean	3½ oz.	9.9	42	0	211
fresh, lean	3½ oz.	7.4	44	0	150
shoulder, lean	2 slices	5.4	30	0	162
shoulder, marbled	2 slices	14.3	55	0	234
pig's feet, pickled	1 oz.	4.6	71	< 1.0	58
rib chop, trimmed	3½ oz.	9.9	43	0	209
rib roast, trimmed	3½ oz.	10.0	44	0	204
sausage					
brown and serve	1 oz.	9.0	82	1.0	98
patty	1	12.0	83	1.0	130
regular link	½ oz.	4.1	62	1.0	60
sirloin, lean, roasted	3½ oz.	10.2	44	0	207
spareribs, roasted	6 medium	35.0	79	0	396
tenderloin, lean, roast	3½ oz.	4.8	28	0	155
top loin chop, trimmed	3½ oz.	7.7	36	0	193
top loin roast, trimmed	3½ oz.	7.5	36	0	187
processed meats					
bacon substitute (breakfast strips)	2 strips	4.8	86	1.0	50
beef breakfast strips	2 strips	7.0	63	1.0	100
beef, chipped	1 oz.	1.1	21	0.4	47
beef jerky	1 oz.	3.6	36	3.3	90
bologna, beef/beef & pork	1 oz.	8.3	83	0.6	90
bratwurst					
pork	2-oz. link	22.0	77	1.8	256
pork & beef	2-oz. link	19.5	78	2.1	226
braunshweiger (pork liver sausage)	1 oz.	5.8	80	0.6	65
chicken roll	1 oz.	1.4	48	0.5	26
corn dog	1	18.9	37	55.8	460
corned beef, jellied	1 oz.	2.9	84	0	31
ham, chopped	1 oz.	3.5	61	0.8	52

	Serving	Total Fat g.	% Cal. from fat	Carbs. in g.	Cal.
hot dog/frank					
beef	1	12.8	81	0.8	142
chicken	1	8.8	68	3.1	116
97% fat-free varieties	1	2.0	30	2.0	60
turkey	1	8.1	71	0.6	102
kielbasa (Polish sausage)	1 oz.	7.1	79	0.6	81
knockwurst/knackwurst	2-oz. link	18.9	81	1.2	209
liver pâté, goose	1 oz.	12.4	85	1.3	131
pepperoni	1 oz.	13.0	83	1.0	140
pork & beef pepperoni	1 oz.	12.5	80	0.8	141
salami					
cooked	1 oz.	7.0	79	< 1.0	80
dry/hard	1 oz.	10.0	75	0	120
sausage					
Italian	2-oz. link	17.7	82	0.4	195
90% fat-free varieties	1 oz.	3.0	66	< 1.0	40
Polish	1-oz. link	8.1	79	0.5	92
smoked	2-oz. link	18.0	85	1.0	190
Vienna	1 sausage	4.0	80	0.3	45
Spam	1 oz.	7.0	79	0.7	80
turkey breast	1 oz.	0.8	23	1.2	31
turkey ham	1 oz.	1.2	32	0.4	34
turkey loaf	1 oz.	2.6	54	0.4	43
turkey pastrami	1 oz.	1.2	33	0.1	33
turkey roll	1 oz.	4.5	56	0.7	72
turkey salami	1 oz.	4.0	72	1.0	50
veal					
arm steak					
lean	3½ oz.	4.8	24	0	180
lean & fat	3½ oz.	19.0	57	0	298
blade					
lean	3½ oz.	8.4	33	0	228
lean & fat	3½ oz.	16.6	54	0	276
breast, stewed	3½ oz.	18.6	65	0	256
chuck, med. fat, braised	3½ oz.	12.8	49	0	235
flank, med. fat, stewed	3½ oz.	32.0	74	0	390
foreshank, med. fat, stewed	3½ oz.	10.4	43	0	216
loin, med. fat, broiled	3½ oz.	13.4	52	0	234
loin chop					
lean	1 chop	4.8	29	0	149
lean & fat	3½ oz.	13.3	48	0	250
plate, med. fat, stewed	3½ oz.	21.2	63	0	303
rib chop					
lean	1 chop	4.6	33	0	125
lean & fat	1 chop	18.4	63	0	264
rump, marbled, roasted	3½ oz.	11.0	44	0	225

	Serving	Total Fat g.	% Cal. from fat	Carbs. in g.	Cal.
sirloin					
lean, roasted	3½ oz.	3.4	17	0	175
marbled, roasted	3½ oz.	6.5	32	0	181
sirloin steak					
lean	3½ oz.	6.0	26	0	204
lean & fat	3½ oz.	20.4	60	0	305

Milk and Yogurt

	Serving	Total Fat g.	% Cal. from fat	Carbs. in g.	Cal.
buttermilk					
1% fat	1 cup	2.2	20	11.7	99
dry	1 T	0.4	14	3.2	25
choc. milk					
2% fat	1 cup	5.0	25	26.0	179
whole	1 cup	8.8	35	30.9	226
condensed milk, sweetened	½ cup	13.2	24	83.2	492
evaporated milk					
skim	½ cup	0.4	4	14.4	100
whole	½ cup	9.5	51	12.7	169
hot cocoa					
low cal, mix w/water	1 cup	0.4	8	8.5	48
mix w/water	1 cup	3.0	23	24.1	120
w/skim milk	1 cup	2.0	11	25.4	158
w/whole milk	1 cup	9.1	38	25.8	218
low-fat milk					
½% fat	1 cup	1.0	10	12.0	90
1% fat	1 cup	2.6	23	11.7	102
1.5% fat/acidophilus	1 cup	4.0	33	12.0	110
2% fat	1 cup	4.7	35	11.7	121
malted milk	1 cup	9.8	37	27.3	237
milkshake					
choc., thick	1 cup	14.0	23	94.0	540
soft serve	1 cup	10.0	27	51.0	334
vanilla, thick	1 cup	14.0	24	88.0	520
Ovaltine, w/1% milk	1 cup	2.6	13	29.7	182
skim milk					
liquid	1 cup	0.4	4	11.9	86
nonfat dry powder	¼ cup	0.2	2	15.6	109
whole milk					
3.5% fat	1 cup	8.2	49	11.4	150
dry powder	¼ cup	8.6	49	12.3	159
yogurt					
coffee/vanilla, low fat	1 cup	2.8	13	31.3	194
frzn, low fat	½ cup	4.3	34	17.9	115
frzn, nonfat	½ cup	0	0	23.0	100
fruit flavored, low fat	1 cup	2.6	10	42.3	225
plain					
low fat	1 cup	4.0	26	15.0	140

	Serving	Total Fat g.	% Cal. from fat	Carbs. in g.	Cal.
skim (nonfat)	1 cup	0	0	17.0	120
whole milk	1 cup	7.4	48	10.6	139

Miscellaneous

Bac o Bits, General Mills	2 t	2.0	72	1.0	25
baking powder	1 t	0	0	0.7	3
baking soda	1 t	0	0	0	0
bouillon cube, beef or chicken	1	0.2	20	1.1	9
chewing gum	1 stick	0	0	2.0	10
choc., baking	1 oz.	15.7	95	8.0	148
cocoa, dry	⅓ cup	3.6	28	12.8	115
honey	1 T	0	0	16.0	64
horseradish, prepared	1 t	0	0	< 1.0	4
icing, decorator	1 t	2.0	26	12.0	70
jam, all varieties	1 T	0	0	12.0	48
jelly, all varieties	1 T	0	0	12.0	48
marmalade, citrus	1 T	0	0	12.0	50
molasses	1 T	0	0	14.0	60
olives					
black	2 large	3.5	97	1.0	36
Greek	3 medium	10.2	96	2.5	96
green	2 medium	1.0	90	0.6	10
pickle relish					
chow chow	1 oz.	0.4	40	1.2	9
sweet	1 T	0.1	5	5.3	19
pickles					
bread & butter	4 slices	0.1	4	5.4	22
dill or sour	1 large	0.1	8	2.7	12
Kosher	1 oz.	0.1	22	0.6	4
sweet	1 oz.	0.4	7	11.6	50
salt	1 t	0	0	0	0
Shake & Bake, Gen. Foods	¼ pkg.	1.7	20	14.0	77
spices/seasonings	1 t	0.2	36	1.4	5
sugar, all varieties	1 T	0	0	11.9	46
sugar substitutes	1 packet	0	0	< 1.0	4
syrup, all varieties	1 T	0	0	15.0	60
vinegar	1 T	0	0	0.9	2
yeast	1 T	0	0	3.0	20

Nuts and Seeds

almond paste	1 T	3.9	55	6.2	64
almonds	12–15	9.3	81	3.5	104
Brazil nuts	4 medium	9.4	91	1.8	93
cashews, roasted	6–8	7.0	74	4.0	85
chestnuts, fresh	3 small	0.6	9	12.9	60
coconut, dried, shredded	⅓ cup	11.0	64	14.8	155

	Serving	Total Fat g.	% Cal. from fat	Carbs. in g.	Cal.
hazelnuts (filberts)	10–12	9.4	80	3.3	106
macadamia nuts, roasted	5 medium	10.9	96	1.9	102
mixed nuts					
w/peanuts	8–12	10.0	83	4.1	109
w/o peanuts	2 T	10.1	83	3.9	110
peanut butter, creamy or chunky	1 T	8.0	76	3.5	94
peanuts					
chopped	2 T	7.0	62	6.8	102
honey roasted	2 T	13.0	78	4.0	150
in shell	1 cup	17.7	76	5.2	209
pecans	2 T	9.2	89	3.2	93
pine nuts (pignolia)	2 T	8.6	88	2.4	88
pistachios	2 T	7.7	75	3.9	92
poppy seeds	1 T	3.9	75	2.1	47
pumpkin seeds	2 T	7.9	76	3.1	93
sesame nut mix	2 T	4.8	66	3.2	65
sesame seeds	2 T	9.0	78	4.2	104
sunflower seeds	2 T	9.5	82	3.4	104
trail mix w/seeds, nuts, carob	2 T	6.0	51	11.0	105
walnuts	2 T	8.1	84	11.7	86

Pasta, Noodles, and Rice

(all measurements after cooking unless otherwise noted)

	Serving	Total Fat g.	% Cal. from fat	Carbs. in g.	Cal.
macaroni					
semolina	1 cup	0.9	4	0.4	197
whole wheat	1 cup	0.8	4	37.2	174
noodles					
Alfredo	1 cup	26.0	46	54.0	506
cellophane, fried	1 cup	4.2	27	24.8	141
chow mein, canned	½ cup	8.0	48	16.0	150
egg	1 cup	2.4	10	39.7	212
manicotti	1 cup	0.4	3	25.8	129
ramen, all varieties	1 cup	8.0	38	26.0	190
rice	1 cup	0.3	2	30.4	140
romanoff	1 cup	22.0	41	56.0	480
rice					
brown	½ cup	0.9	7	22.4	108
fried	½ cup	5.0	28	25.0	160
long grain & wild	½ cup	2.1	16	22.5	120
pilaf	½ cup	6.0	28	30.0	190
Spanish style	½ cup	0.4	3	25.7	120
white	½ cup	0.2	1	29.3	133
spaghetti, enriched	1 cup	0.9	4	39.7	197

	Serving	Total Fat g.	% Cal. from fat	Carbs. in g.	Cal.
Poultry					
chicken					
breast					
w/skin, fried	½ breast	8.7	36	1.6	218
w/o skin, fried	½ breast	4.1	23	0.4	161
w/skin, roasted	½ breast	7.6	35	0	193
w/o skin, roasted	½ breast	3.1	20	0	142
fryers					
w/skin, batter dipped, fried	3½ oz.	17.4	54	9.4	289
w/o skin, fried	3½ oz.	11.6	44	2.6	239
w/skin, roasted	3½ oz.	13.6	51	0	239
w/o skin, roasted	3½ oz.	7.4	35	0	190
giblets, fried	3½ oz.	13.5	44	4.4	277
gizzard, simmered	3½ oz.	4.8	27	1.0	157
heart, simmered	3½ oz.	7.9	38	0.1	185
leg					
w/skin, fried	1 leg	16.2	51	2.8	285
w/skin, roasted	1 leg	15.4	52	0	265
w/o skin, roasted	1 leg	8.1	39	0	187
liver, simmered	3½ oz.	5.5	31	0.9	157
roll, light meat	3½ oz.	7.4	42	2.5	159
stewers					
w/skin	3½ oz.	18.9	60	0	285
w/o skin	3½ oz.	11.9	45	0	237
thigh					
w/skin, fried	1 thigh	9.3	52	2.0	162
w/skin, roasted	1 thigh	9.6	0	56	153
w/o skin, roasted	1 thigh	5.7	47	0	109
wing					
w/skin, fried	1 wing	7.1	62	0.8	103
w/skin, roasted	1 wing	6.6	60	0	99
duck					
w/skin, roasted	3½ oz.	28.4	76	0	337
w/o skin, roasted	3½ oz.	11.2	50	0	201
turkey					
breast					
barbecued, Louis Rich	3½ oz.	3.2	24	3.7	118
oven roasted, Louis Rich	3½ oz.	3.2	26	1.7	111
smoked, Louis Rich	3½ oz.	3.7	28	0.9	118
dark meat					
w/skin, roasted	3½ oz.	11.5	47	0	221
w/o skin, roasted	3½ oz.	7.2	35	0	187
ground	3½ oz.	13.3	55	0	219
ham, cured	3½ oz.	5.1	36	0.4	128
light meat					
w/skin, roasted	3½ oz.	9.7	42	0	208
w/o skin, roasted	3½ oz.	5.0	26	0	170

	Serving	Total Fat g.	% Cal. from fat	Carbs. in g.	Cal.
loaf, breast meat	3½ oz.	1.6	13	0	110
patties, breaded/fried	1 patty	16.9	57	14.8	266
roll, light meat	3½ oz.	7.2	44	0.5	147
sausage, cooked	1 oz.	3.6	57	0.1	57
sliced w/gravy, frzn	5 oz.	3.7	35	6.6	95
wing drumettes, smoked, Louis Rich	3½ oz.	7.7	39	0.4	178

Salad Dressings

	Serving	Total Fat g.	% Cal. from fat	Carbs. in g.	Cal.
blue cheese					
fat free	1 T	0	0	5.0	20
low cal	1 T	1.9	63	1.7	27
regular	1 T	8.0	94	1.1	77
buttermilk, from mix	1 T	5.8	90	1.2	58
Caesar	1 T	8.0	94	0.8	76
French					
creamy	1 T	6.9	89	1.9	70
fat free	1 T	0	0	3.0	18
low cal	1 T	0.9	37	3.5	22
regular	1 T	6.4	86	2.7	67
garlic, from mix	1 T	9.2	97	0.5	85
honey mustard	1 T	6.6	67	7.1	89
Italian					
creamy	1 T	5.5	92	1.4	54
fat free	1 T	0	0	1.5	6
low cal	1 T	1.5	84	0.7	16
regular zesty, from mix	1 T	9.2	97	0.6	85
Kraft Free	1 T	0	0	5.0	20
Kraft, reduced cal	1 T	1.0	36	4.0	25
mayonnaise type					
low cal	1 T	1.8	85	0.7	19
regular	1 T	4.9	77	3.5	57
oil & vinegar	1 T	7.5	98	0.4	69
ranch style, prep. w/mayo	1 T	6.0	95	1.0	58
Russian					
low cal	1 T	0.7	26	4.5	24
regular	1 T	7.8	92	1.6	76
sesame seed	1 T	6.9	91	1.3	68
sweet & sour	1 T	0.9	28	5.2	29
Thousand Island					
fat free	1 T	0	0	5.0	20
low cal	1 T	1.6	60	2.5	24
regular	1 T	5.6	85	2.4	59

Snack Foods

	Serving	Total Fat g.	% Cal. from fat	Carbs. in g.	Cal.
bagel chips or crisps	1 oz.	4.0	36	13.0	100
Bugles	1 oz.	8.0	48	18.0	150
Cheese Puff balls	1 oz.	10.6	59	16.0	161

	Serving	Total Fat g.	% Cal. from fat	Carbs. in g.	Cal.
Cheese Puffs, Cheetos	1 oz.	10.0	56	17.0	160
cheese straws	4 pieces	7.2	59	8.3	109
corn chips, Frito's, regular	1 oz.	10.0	56	15.0	160
corn nuts, all flavors	1 oz.	4.0	28	20.0	130
Cracker Jack	1 oz.	3.0	23	22.0	120
party mix (cereal, pretzels, nuts)	1 cup	23.0	66	22.3	312
popcorn					
air popped	1 cup	0.3	8	6.3	31
caramel	1 cup	4.5	27	27.9	152
microwave, "lite"	1 cup	1.0	33	4.6	27
microwave, plain	1 cup	3.3	67	4.0	44
microwave, w/butter	1 cup	4.5	66	6.8	61
popped w/oil	1 cup	3.1	51	6.2	55
pork rinds, Frito-Lay	1 oz.	8.9	52	0	154
potato chips					
individually	10 chips	8.0	64	9.1	113
by weight	1 oz.	9.8	58	15.0	152
barbecue flavor	1 oz.	9.2	59	15.0	139
light, Pringles	1 oz.	8.0	48	17.0	150
regular, Pringles	1 oz.	12.0	63	12.0	170
potato sticks	1 oz.	9.8	59	15.1	148
pretzels	1 oz.	1.0	8	22.5	108
rice cakes	1	0	10	7.0	35
tortilla chips					
Doritos	1 oz.	7.0	45	18.0	140
no oil, baked	1 oz.	1.5	12	24.0	110
Tostitos	1 oz.	8.0	48	17.0	150

Soups

	Serving	Total Fat g.	% Cal. from fat	Carbs. in g.	Cal.
asparagus					
cream of, w/milk	1 cup	8.2	46	16.4	161
cream of, w/water	1 cup	4.1	42	10.4	87
bean					
w/bacon	1 cup	5.9	31	22.8	173
w/franks	1 cup	7.0	34	22.0	187
w/ham	1 cup	8.5	33	27.1	231
w/o meat	1 cup	1.0	7	24.7	130
beef					
broth	1 cup	0.1	6	0.6	14
chunky	1 cup	5.1	27	19.6	171
beef barley	1 cup	1.0	15	10.0	59
beef noodle	1 cup	3.1	33	9.0	84
black bean	1 cup	1.5	11	19.8	116
broccoli, creamy, w/water	1 cup	2.8	37	9.3	69
Campbell's Chunky					
w/meat	1 cup	5.1	27	19.6	171
w/o meat	1 cup	3.7	27	19.0	122

	Serving	Total Fat g.	% Cal. from fat	Carbs. in g.	Cal.
Campbell's Healthy Request					
chicken, cream of, w/water	1 cup	2.0	26	11.0	70
mushroom, cream of, w/water	1 cup	2.0	30	9.0	60
tomato, w/water	1 cup	2.0	20	17.0	90
canned vegetable type, w/o meat	1 cup	1.6	24	9.0	59
chicken					
chunky	1 cup	6.0	32	19.0	170
cream of, w/milk	1 cup	11.5	42	15.0	191
cream of, w/water	1 cup	7.4	57	9.3	116
chicken & dumplings	1 cup	2.8	33	8.7	76
chicken & stars	1 cup	1.8	29	6.5	55
chicken & wild rice	1 cup	2.0	23	12.4	80
chicken gumbo	1 cup	1.4	23	8.4	56
chicken mushroom	1 cup	9.2	63	9.3	132
chicken noodle					
chunky	1 cup	5.2	31	14.9	149
w/water	1 cup	2.5	30	9.4	75
chicken vegetable					
chunky	1 cup	4.8	26	18.9	167
w/water	1 cup	2.8	34	8.6	74
chicken w/rice					
chunky	1 cup	3.2	23	13.0	127
w/water	1 cup	1.9	29	7.2	60
clam chowder					
Manhattan chunky	1 cup	3.4	23	18.8	133
New England	1 cup	6.6	4	16.6	163
consommé w/gelatin	1 cup	0	0	1.8	29
crab	1 cup	1.5	18	10.3	76
dehydrated					
asparagus, cream of	1 cup	1.7	26	9.0	59
bean w/bacon	1 cup	2.2	19	16.4	105
beef broth cube	1 cube	0.5	32	1.4	14
beef noodle	1 cup	0.7	15	1.9	41
cauliflower	1 cup	1.7	23	10.7	68
chicken, cream of	1 cup	5.3	45	13.4	107
chicken broth cube	1 cube	0.2	20	1.1	9
chicken noodle	1 cup	1.2	20	7.4	53
chicken rice	1 cup	1.4	21	9.3	60
clam chowder					
Manhattan	1 cup	2.0	23	13.0	80
New England	1 cup	2.0	26	12.0	70
minestrone	1 cup	1.7	19	11.9	79
mushroom	1 cup	4.9	46	11.1	96
onion					
dry mix	1 pkg.	2.3	18	20.9	115
prepared	1 cup	0.5	17	4.7	27
tomato	1 cup	2.4	21	19.4	102
vegetable beef	1 cup	1.1	19	8.0	53

	Serving	Total Fat g.	% Cal. from fat	Carbs. in g.	Cal.
gazpacho w/o fat	1 cup	0.2	4	8.8	41
hmde or restaurant style					
celery, cream of, w/whole milk	1 cup	9.7	53	14.5	164
chicken broth	1 cup	1.4	33	60	38
clam chowder					
Manhattan	1 cup	2.0	23	13.0	80
New England	1 cup	9.0	43	16.0	188
corn chowder, traditional	1 cup	15.0	45	36.0	298
gazpacho, traditional	1 cup	7.0	63	8.7	100
onion, French, w/o cheese	1 cup	5.8	46	14.4	114
oyster stew, w/whole milk	1 cup	8.0	54	9.8	134
lentil	1 cup	2.1	10	29.9	181
minestrone					
chunky	1 cup	2.8	20	20.7	127
w/water	1 cup	2.5	27	11.2	83
mushroom, cream of					
condensed	1 can	23.1	66	22.6	313
w/milk	1 cup	13.6	60	15.0	203
w/water	1 cup	9.0	63	9.3	129
mushroom barley	1 cup	1.7	18	14.3	84
mushroom w/beef stock	1 cup	4.0	42	9.3	85
onion	1 cup	1.7	27	8.2	57
oyster stew, w/water	1 cup	3.8	58	4.1	59
pea					
green, w/water	1 cup	2.9	16	26.5	164
split	1 cup	0.8	5	23.6	143
split w/ham	1 cup	4.4	21	28.0	189
potato, cream of, w/milk	1 cup	6.5	39	17.2	148
shrimp, cream of, w/milk	1 cup	9.3	51	13.9	165
tomato					
w/milk	1 cup	6.0	34	22.3	160
w/water	1 cup	1.9	20	16.6	86
tomato beef w/noodle	1 cup	4.3	28	21.2	140
tomato bisque w/milk	1 cup	6.6	30	29.4	198
tomato rice	1 cup	2.7	20	21.9	120
turkey, chunky	1 cup	5.1	36	13.7	128
turkey noodle	1 cup	2.0	26	8.6	69
turkey vegetable	1 cup	3.0	36	8.6	74
vegetable, chunky	1 cup	3.7	27	19.0	122
vegetable w/beef, chunky	1 cup	3.7	24	14.1	141
vegetable w/beef broth	1 cup	1.9	22	10.2	79
vegetarian vegetable	1 cup	1.2	15	13.3	73
wonton	1 cup	1.0	23	4.6	40

Vegetables

	Serving	Total Fat g.	% Cal. from fat	Carbs. in g.	Cal.
alfalfa sprouts, raw	½ cup	0.1	18	0.7	5
artichoke, boiled	1 medium	0.2	3	13.4	53

220

	Serving	Total Fat g.	% Cal. from fat	Carbs. in g.	Cal.
artichoke hearts, boiled	½ cup	0.1	2	8.7	37
asparagus, cooked	½ cup	0.3	12	3.8	22
avocado					
California	1 (6 oz.)	30.0	88	12.0	306
Florida	1 (11 oz.)	27.0	72	27.1	339
bamboo shoots, raw	½ cup	0.2	9	4.0	21
beans					
all types, cooked w/o fat	½ cup	0.4	3	16.7	143
baked, brown sugar & molasses	½ cup	1.5	10	24.2	132
baked, vegetarian	½ cup	0.6	5	26.1	118
baked w/pork & tomato sauce	½ cup	1.3	9	24.5	123
homestyle, canned	½ cup	1.6	11	23.9	132
beets, pickled	½ cup	0.1	1	18.6	75
black-eyed peas (cowpeas), cooked	½ cup	0.6	5	17.3	100
broccoli					
cooked	½ cup	0.3	12	4.0	22
frzn, chopped, cooked	½ cup	0.1	4	4.9	25
frzn in butter sauce	½ cup	2.0	45	5.9	40
frzn w/cheese sauce	½ cup	6.2	48	11.6	116
raw	½ cup	0.2	15	2.3	12
brussels sprouts, cooked	½ cup	0.4	12	6.8	30
butter beans, canned	½ cup	0.4	5	15.9	76
cabbage					
Chinese, raw	1 cup	0.2	18	1.6	10
green, cooked	½ cup	0.1	6	3.6	16
red, raw, shredded	½ cup	0.1	9	2.1	10
carrot					
cooked	½ cup	0.1	3	8.2	35
raw	1 large	0.1	3	7.3	31
cauliflower					
cooked	1 cup	0.2	6	5.8	30
frzn w/cheese sauce	½ cup	6.1	48	11.7	114
raw	1 cup	0.1	7	2.5	12
celery					
cooked	½ cup	0.1	7	3.0	13
raw	1 stalk	0.1	15	1.5	6
chard, cooked	½ cup	0.1	5	3.6	18
chiles, green	¼ cup	0	0	2.0	10
Chinese-style vegetables, frzn	½ cup	4.0	49	7.4	74
chives, raw, chopped	1 T	0	0	0.1	1
collard greens, cooked	½ cup	0.1	5	3.9	17
corn					
corn on the cob	1 medium	1.0	7	28.7	120
cream style, canned	½ cup	0.5	5	23.2	93
frzn, cooked	½ cup	0.1	1	16.8	67
frzn w/butter sauce	½ cup	2.2	18	21.8	110
whole kernel, cooked	½ cup	1.1	11	20.6	89

	Serving	Total Fat g.	% Cal. from fat	Carbs. in g.	Cal.
cucumber					
w/skin	½ medium	0.2	9	4.4	20
w/o skin, sliced	½ cup	0.1	13	1.5	7
dandelion greens, cooked	½ cup	0.3	16	3.3	17
eggplant, cooked	½ cup	0.1	7	3.2	13
endive lettuce	1 cup	0.2	23	1.6	8
garbanzo beans (chickpeas), cooked	½ cup	2.1	14	22.5	135
green beans					
French style, cooked	½ cup	0.2	7	5.9	26
snap, cooked	½ cup	0.2	8	4.9	22
hominy, white or yellow, cooked	1 cup	0.7	5	30.0	138
kale, cooked	½ cup	0.3	13	3.7	21
kidney beans, red, cooked	½ cup	0.5	4	20.2	112
leeks, chopped, raw	¼ cup	0.1	6	3.7	16
lentils, cooked	½ cup	0.4	3	19.9	116
lettuce, leaf	1 cup	0.2	18	2.0	10
lima beans, cooked	½ cup	0.4	3	19.7	108
miso (soybean product)	½ cup	8.4	27	38.6	284
mushrooms					
canned	½ cup	0.2	9	3.9	19
fried/sautéed	4 medium	7.4	85	1.4	78
raw	½ cup	0.2	20	1.6	9
mustard greens, cooked	½ cup	0.2	16	1.5	11
okra, cooked	½ cup	0.1	4	5.8	25
onions, chopped, raw	½ cup	0.1	3	6.9	30
parsley, chopped, raw	¼ cup	0.1	18	0.9	5
parsnips, cooked	½ cup	0.2	3	15.2	63
peas, green, cooked	½ cup	0.2	3	12.5	67
pepper, bell, chopped, raw	½ cup	0.1	7	3.2	13
pimientos, canned	1 oz.	0	0	2.0	10
potato					
au gratin					
from mix	½ cup	6.0	39	19.0	140
hmde	½ cup	9.3	52	13.7	160
baked w/skin	1 medium	0.2	1	51.0	220
boiled w/o skin	½ cup	0.1	1	27.0	116
french fries					
frzn	10 pieces	4.4	36	17.0	111
hmde	10 pieces	8.3	47	20.0	158
hash browns	½ cup	10.9	60	16.6	163
mashed					
from flakes, w/milk & marg.	½ cup	6.0	41	17.0	130
w/milk & marg.	½ cup	4.4	36	17.5	111
pan fried, O'Brien	½ cup	15.0	58	24.8	231
potato pancakes	1 cake	12.6	48	26.4	237
potato puffs, frzn, prep. w/oil	½ cup	6.7	44	18.9	138

	Serving	Total Fat g.	% Cal. from fat	Carbs. in g.	Cal.
scalloped					
from mix	1 serving	5.9	42	17.5	127
hmde	½ cup	4.5	39	13.2	105
w/cheese	½ cup	9.7	49	13.4	177
twice-baked potato, w/cheese	1 medium	9.9	49	18.2	180
pumpkin, canned	½ cup	0.3	6	9.9	41
radish, raw	10	0.2	26	1.6	7
rhubarb, raw	1 cup	0.2	6	7.0	29
sauerkraut, canned	½ cup	0.2	8	5.1	22
scallions, raw	5 medium	0.2	3	13.0	60
soybeans, mature, cooked	½ cup	7.7	47	8.6	149
spinach					
cooked	½ cup	0.2	9	3.4	21
creamed	½ cup	5.1	58	6.8	79
raw	1 cup	0.2	15	2.0	12
squash					
acorn					
baked	½ cup	0.1	2	14.9	57
mashed w/o fat	½ cup	0.1	2	10.7	41
butternut, cooked	½ cup	0.1	2	10.7	41
summer					
cooked	½ cup	0.3	15	3.9	18
raw, slice	½ cup	0.1	7	2.8	13
winter, cooked	½ cup	0.6	14	8.9	39
succotash, cooked	½ cup	0.8	7	23.4	111
sweet potato					
baked	1 small	0.1	1	27.7	118
candied	½ cup	3.4	21	29.3	144
mashed w/o fat	½ cup	0.5	3	39.8	172
tempeh (soybean product)	½ cup	6.4	35	14.1	165
tofu (soybean curd), raw, firm	4 oz.	4.0	40	4.0	90
tomato					
boiled	½ cup	0.5	14	7.0	32
raw	1 medium	0.4	14	5.7	26
stewed	½ cup	0.2	5	8.3	34
tomato paste, canned	½ cup	1.2	10	24.7	110
turnip greens, cooked	½ cup	0.2	12	3.1	15
turnips, cooked	½ cup	0.1	6	3.8	14
water chestnuts, canned, sliced	½ cup	0	0	8.7	35
watercress, raw	½ cup	0	0	0.2	2
wax beans, canned	½ cup	0.2	7	4.5	25
yam, boiled/baked	½ cup	0.1	1	18.8	79
zucchini, cooked	½ cup	0.1	6	3.5	14

Vegetable Salads

	Serving	Total Fat g.	% Cal. from fat	Carbs. in g.	Cal.
carrot-raisin salad	½ cup	5.8	34	27.9	153
chef salad w/o dressing	1 cup	4.2	58	2.5	65

	Serving	Total Fat g.	% Cal. from fat	Carbs. in g.	Cal.
coleslaw					
w/mayo-type dressing	½ cup	10.5	68	11.1	140
w/vinaigrette	½ cup	3.0	35	10.7	78
macaroni salad w/mayo	½ cup	12.8	58	20.8	200
potato salad					
German style	½ cup	3.0	23	23.0	120
w/mayo dressing	½ cup	10.3	52	14.0	179
salad bar items					
alfalfa sprouts	2 T	0	0	0.5	2
bacon bits	1 T	1.0	43	0	21
beets, pickled	2 T	0	0	4.5	18
broccoli, raw	2 T	0	0	0.6	3
carrots, raw	2 T	0	0	0.3	6
cheese, shredded	2 T	4.6	74	0.2	56
chickpeas	2 T	0.3	8	6.8	36
cottage cheese	½ cup	5.1	39	3.0	116
croutons	½ oz.	2.6	38	8.0	62
cucumber	2 T	0	0	0.4	2
eggs, cooked, chopped	2 T	1.9	63	0.2	27
lettuce	½ cup	0	0	0.8	4
mushrooms, raw	2 T	0	0	0.3	2
onion, raw	2 T	0.1	12	1.5	7
pepper, green, raw	2 T	0	0	0.7	3
potato salad	½ cup	10.3	52	14.0	179
tomato, raw	2 slices	0	0	0.4	2
tabbouli salad	½ cup	9.5	49	18.0	173
taco salad w/taco sauce	1 cup	15.3	61	13.2	226
three-bean salad	½ cup	8.2	51	15.5	145
Waldorf salad w/mayo	½ cup	12.7	73	9.1	157